Horses Adored and Men Endured

a memoir of falling and getting back up

Susan Friedland

D1600623

Horses Adored and Men Endured

Saddle Seeks Horse Press

In this memoir some names have been changed to protect the privacy of individuals.

Cover Design: Amy Summer Ellison
Editor: Holly Caccamise
Photos: Kerri Weiss Photography
Author Photo and Original "You should write a book!" Encourager: Carolyn Rikje

ISBN: 978-1-7327105-1-1
Print Edition

Susan Friedland
North Tustin, California
saddleseekshorse.com

Praise for *Horses Adored and Men Endured*

"Susan Friedland writes with a level of sophistication that brings form to the confounding realm of dating. Just like the unsuccessful ride that ends in falling off, the unsuccessful date is often not funny until it drifts into the past. Only then, can we laugh at the utter silliness of it. Susan's stories will have you smiling, as they collectively establish one unique complication for horsewomen searching out a life partner: the Horse might be more attractive than the Knight."

Jean Abernethy
Creator of Fergus the Horse

"If you enjoy her *Saddle Seeks Horse* blog as much as I do, you'll love getting to know Susan Friedland even better in her memoir. Susan takes readers behind the scenes of her life as she deals with the trials and tribulations of horse ownership and the search for true love. An entertaining read!"

Carly Kade
Author of the *In the Reins* series

"I've been following along with Susan's blog, *Saddle Seeks Horse* from the beginning of its existence. I've loved every blog post about Susan and Knight's ever-changing journey. It was a treat to sit down and learn how Susan finally found her perfect match. Just like horse shopping, finding Mr. Right is filled with a lot of laughs and some defeat along the way. Unicorns and Mr. Right do exist! Order your favorite chai latte and get ready to feel like you are catching up with your best friend and her romantic journey."

Raquel Lynn
Blogger behind *Horses & Heels* and *Stable Style*

Susan Friedland

HORSES ADORED AND MEN ENDURED

Susan Friedland, an award-winning equestrian blogger at Saddle Seeks Horse, is a middle school teacher by day and horse girl 24/7. The displaced Midwesterner now residing in California, charms blog readers with a glimpse of the real horse life featuring alfalfa in her handbag, always-dusty tall boots, and product reviews for horse and rider. Susan's writing about horses and the people who love them has been featured in *Horse Illustrated*, *Sidelines*, *Modern Luxury Scottsdale* and on the websites *Equik-trekking*, *Horse Nation* and *Horse Channel*. Check out the blog *Saddle Seeks Horse* and feel free to connect if you ever want to talk horse.

saddleseekshorse.com
susan@saddleseekshorse.com

Dedication and Gratitude

Thank you Mom and Dad!
You're my first and fiercest fans.
1400 kisses and hugs are coming your way soon.

This book is dedicated to anyone who has experienced a steady stream of bad dates and felt like giving up on love.

This book is for anyone who has ever loved, lived for or longed for a horse. I totally get you.

Contents

PART I

Green as Grass

CHAPTER 1

Not "Our" Night

WHEN I WAS a girl of 10, newly smitten with horse fever, I wasn't interested in boys and thought it would be perfect if only I could marry a horse.

Two decades later I sometimes feared I might, in fact, have to marry a horse. There seemed to be no suitable human alternative . . . as evidenced by the blind date standing at my door wearing an orangey leather jacket.

"I like your sconces," he smiled.

Did I hear that right? Seriously!? He liked my sconces? What about my hair? My outfit?

The wrought iron sconces flanking a large floral print over the sofa in my Los Angeles starter apartment captured Kevin's attention the moment he stepped inside. I had only just learned what sconces were a few years before when Pottery Barn began mailing me catalogs.

Minutes earlier when I opened the door and saw him standing there, I just *knew* it wasn't going to work out between us, and I hoped my face didn't display my disappointment.

Kevin was not my physical ideal—at all. And I couldn't get past the orangey leather jacket. Those factors combined with the sconce compliment threw me off.

I had a sixth sense it was going to be a long night.

My friend Audrey who was in a rock band and cut hair for her day job set us up. I had been to one of her performances wearing my new, flashy lime green corduroy jacket. Something about having moved to California from Illinois the year before made me kick up my fashion spunkiness a notch. I ditched my Midwestern grays and numerous wool turtlenecks in favor of the vivid green and the colors and fabrics of summer.

From across the dusky room I had apparently made quite an impression on Kevin. The next time he got a haircut from Audrey he asked if he could be introduced to the girl in the green jacket he had laid eyes on at the concert.

I said yes to Audrey's request to give Kevin my number, and yes again when he called me to ask me out.

Kevin showed up to my door wearing a jacket that looked like something worn by a character from the 1970s sitcom *Good Times*. It was the late 1990s, and the only people who were able to wear a clearly out of style jacket and look vintage, thus making the jacket hip, were celebrities or people gorgeous enough they might be mistaken for a celebrity. Kevin was neither.

We began the date at a Starbucks, exchanging niceties over lattes about where we grew up, went to college, and attended church. In addition to the lack of physical attraction, there was very little personality attraction either, but I kept up a cordial conversation because it was my only option.

After Starbucks we went to The Whiskey, a Hollywood club. As he drove the winding roads of Laurel Canyon down into Hollywood, Kevin asked, "So, have you ever been to Hollywood before?"

It seemed just because I was from the Midwest, people in California assumed I was sheltered. I felt his question was slightly condescending.

"Yes, I've lived in L.A. over a year now, and my job takes me to Hollywood once in a while. And I've been there with friends."

We kept the awkward conversation going until we arrived, and Kevin handed the keys to the valet. Off we went into the dark cavern of musical entertainment, where I learned something from what happened next: It's *never* a good idea to go to a concert on a blind date. There's nothing more miserable than sitting in cramped quarters with a virtual stranger listening to music you don't know, trying to shout above the noise to carry on a conversation. In hindsight it would have been more pleasant to go to the dentist.

The first band to take the stage was a heavy metal Christian band, which was not my preferred genre. The next act was a ska band who were members of a local youth group, and it showed. This band was a definite improvement over the metal band, but after a while, all ska music sounds alike with its islandy beat and bursts of trumpet and trombone.

As I sat in the dark balcony next to my date—who

was really the belle of the ball, hobnobbing with dozens of people who all seemed to actually enjoy the music—I realized I was tired, bored and ready to go home.

My brain provided an escape, allowing me to tolerate the seemingly unending date. As the bands rocked, I envisioned myself riding my horse, jumping a course in a rhythmical canter, navigating various combinations of colorful fences.

I thought about my barn self saturated with the aroma of horse and hay, sporting dirt under my fingernails—that was the true me. The young woman on the blind date at the hip club in Hollywood wasn't really me.

Dating was awkward and not a fun activity in spite of what the movies depicted. Yet I knew I had to have an open mind about meeting people if I ever wanted to find that special someone. Even though I was more at home at the stable where my horse lived, it was not a promising venue in which to meet the man of my dreams. Most of my fellow riders were middle-aged women. There were a few men, but they were either old enough to be my dad or gay.

The show ended around midnight, and when Kevin and I walked out to meet the valet, he told us he was sorry but he had accidentally locked the keys in the car.

Kevin held a large golf umbrella over us as it had started to mist. There we were in Tinsel Town, under an umbrella with the lights of Sunset Boulevard flickering at us, Kevin in his orangey jacket, I in my green. What a moment it could have been.

"Can you get them out?" Kevin asked.

The valet said sorry and shook his head.

Kevin stood there defeated and passive.

Something in me took over. "Look, you locked the keys in the car," I said. "You're the one who needs to get them out. Call a locksmith. We can't stand here all night in the rain!" What I was really thinking was, *Help! I'm having a miserable night and I don't want this guy to be under any illusion this is a romantic moment. I doooon't like him.*

The valet called for a locksmith, but Kevin and I had to wait about 20 minutes under the umbrella until he arrived. My brain has graciously blocked out the umbrella conversation, because one woman can only sustain so much awkward in one night. When the locksmith opened the door and retrieved the car keys, I felt a surge of relief and probably should have kissed *him* under the Hollywood sky.

For the first half of the car ride home, I resented Kevin for not taking charge of the key situation. But at least we were on our way, no longer standing in what could have been a perfectly romantic situation with the right man, huddled under an umbrella on Sunset Boulevard at midnight in the rain. Around the halfway point to my apartment when I was perking up thinking about exiting this situation and throwing on my flannel pajamas, Kevin interrupted my thoughts.

"Uh, oh! Oh, no!"

He looked into his rear view mirror and started slowing down. "I'm being pulled over." He eased the car to the side of the freeway, and I turned and saw red flashing lights.

"What happened? You weren't speeding."

"I know what this is about."

Yikes! What did that mean?

An officer approached Kevin's window, shined his flashlight into the car and snapped, "Do you know why I stopped you?"

"No, officer."

Wasn't that technically a lie since he had just said he knew what this was about? Definitely not marriage material. I felt less guilty for judging the orangey jacket.

"You're driving with expired tags on your license plate. I need to see your driver's license and proof of insurance."

Kevin rifled through his glove compartment and center console. The officer looked impatient.

"Sorry, officer, I can't seem to find them." Kevin moaned and slumped as the officer stepped away for a few minutes. I was still trying to interpret the comment, *I know what this is about.*

The officer returned, "Mr. Smalley, your license has been suspended. Does that ring a bell? And it appears in addition to having expired tags and driving without a license, you do not currently have car insurance. Do you realize how serious this is?"

Kevin said yes, looking down. He offered an excuse about having been involved in an auto accident and having to go to court.

"Mr. Smalley, do you realize because of your infractions, I have the legal right to impound this vehicle and take you to jail tonight? But I don't want to do that right now in front of your lady friend."

Officer, I'm NOT his lady friend; I'm not even a friend! I'm an innocent bystander on the world's worst blind date ever. You should have seen how he handled the keys being locked in the car, I thought.

The officer continued, "I'm going to cite you, and you'll need to appear in court. And because you don't have a license, she'll have to drive home." The officer walked away to write up the ticket.

Kevin sat there helplessly. He looked like he was going to cry, but then turned to me with a forced smile, "This just isn't our night is it?"

I thought, *This isn't OUR anything. There is no OUR! OUR implies togetherness. We are not together!*

"You know, one of my personality flaws is I'm just a really laid-back person. I know I should have taken care of this before," Kevin rationalized.

"There are certain situations in life you can't afford to be laid back about," I said firmly. "Having a valid license, current tags for your plate and auto insurance fall into that category!"

I felt a little better after my mini lecture.

The police officer returned, handing over the citation. He then made sure we swapped positions in the front seat. I became the driver of Kevin's red Jetta. Thank God it was not stick shift or I don't think we would have ever made it home.

We drove in silence the remaining 10 miles to my apartment building. Once we arrived I asked Kevin how he was going to make it home since he wasn't allowed to drive his car.

Kevin climbed back into the driver's seat and said he *was* going to drive home because it wasn't far.

"I'd like to see you again," Kevin said.

I said something to acknowledge his request but not encourage any future dates. Something like, "Oh."

I've read a respected relationship author who says you should give each person you date a minimum of five dates. I respectfully disagree. Some dates aren't worth five minutes of time. Sometimes you just know. This was one of those times.

The next time I saw my hairstylist friend she was very apologetic. I assured her it wasn't her fault, and said even if it weren't for the police officer getting involved, I don't think it would have been a love match anyway.

I didn't tell her the part about the odd sconce compliment, or the orangey leather jacket.

Even though that date was a fiasco and I was still single and not on a bridal path, at least I had a tall, dark, and handsome horse to be my companion on the bridle path.

And that realization brought a small measure of comfort to my disappointed heart.

CHAPTER 2

The Pinto and the Headless Horseman

IN THIRD GRADE I bought a book from the Scholastic Book Fair titled *The Pony Problem*. It was a paperback about a girl who won a pony from a magazine as a result of winning the "Name this Pony and Win it for Your Very Own" contest. She entered the name Hopscotch, and a few weeks later, a buckskin mare was delivered to the door of her boxy suburban home. The main character strung up a laundry line around trees in the front yard to make a small paddock to contain her beautiful prize. The neighbors caused a ruckus and the drama began, because as everyone knows, you can't have a pony or horse in your front yard in the suburbs.

I learned that wasn't entirely true because later that year, the Headless Horseman appeared around dusk in front of my family's yellow ranch home on Virginia Drive. The black-caped rider on a black and white pinto held up a plastic doll's head on a stick and walked down the street. The eerie clip clop of hooves on the pavement and the purposefully slow pace of the horse made it seem like the rider was a lone member of a funeral procession from centuries ago. What made this so unusual is our house was located smack in the middle of a small town with small houses on small lots—unsuitable for horses, like in the book *The Pony Problem*.

I found out the Halloween rider wasn't *the* Headless Horseman, but my sister Renee's high school friend. Jannee boarded her horse a couple of blocks away from us in the backyard of an unusually large lot—one zoned to accommodate a backyard horse.

The pinto's name was Mandy, and I'll never forget the spring day Jannee, sans creepy costume, rode the pretty mare back over to our house. Mandy trotted up onto our lawn. *Would mom and dad allow this?* I wondered.

My life was about to change forever.

Because they were older and friends with Jannee, my sisters got to ride first. It seemed like forever, and then finally it was my turn. Jannee boosted me up onto Mandy's back and let me ride her around *without* someone else holding onto the bridle. Before that point in my life, I had only been on pony rides, where a teenager led me around. It was fun, yet tame; nice, but not overly exciting. I just kind of sat there holding onto the saddle horn.

Before I started my solo ride in our backyard next to the tulip tree, I got a quick lesson from Jannee on neck reining. "When you rest the reins against her neck, she'll turn in that direction. If you lean them toward the right side, she'll go right. If you want to go left, rest them left."

I learned how to kick to make Mandy go, and off we

went on a few laps around the perimeter of our yard. I practiced my steering around random trees and bushes. My dad did not believe in symmetry in landscaping, and if a squirrel buried a walnut in the ground and it later sprouted, my dad would let it burst forth into a baby tree. All the better to circle around and work on my riding cues.

By the end of the ride, something had clicked inside of me. As I sat tall in the western saddle, I was transformed from a shy bookworm to a proud cowgirl. Soon my kitty folders would be replaced with horse folders, and our picnic table benches would be transformed into horse show jumps. Our backyard would become a riding arena in which I would walk, trot and canter my imaginary mount and do figures of 8. My stuffed animal shelves made way for the bay Running Stallion, Running Mare, Running Foal and other members of the Breyer model horse family.

I had contracted an incurable case of horse fever, and I would never be the same.

CHAPTER 3

Horse Hope Chest

IN FIFTH GRADE I created a hope chest. I'm not sure if hope chests are all the rage anymore, but my older sisters had hope chests. These were cedar chests in which brides-to-be put household items they were saving up for when they would be whisked away by their dashing fiancé to enter a life of marital bliss. The goal was to gather supplies such as mixing bowls and cutting boards so the young bride would be fully equipped and ready to keep house. The chest was more than just a depository; it was a tangible symbol of the dream to be a wife.

My hope chest was one of a kind. And it had nothing to do with boys or men or getting married.

I had a *horse* hope chest. My loftiest dream was to one day ride off into the sunset on a white Arabian. Or black. Or any other color. And in reality, I would have been happy with any horse standing on four legs.

My hope chest wasn't like my sister Renee's Lane oak creation with a country blue plaid seat. It was a cardboard box with the words "Horse Hope Chest" scrawled in black marker. It contained wonderful treasures acquired from occasional visits to Farm and Fleet and Blanchard's Feed and Stable Supply. My hope chest housed a silver sweat scraper, hoof pick, rubber curry comb, stiff dandy brush, a sponge and a container of Lexol leather conditioner—all the amenities a girl would need for when she finally had a horse of her own.

The most prized possession of my hope chest was an old-fashioned western bridle with a curb bit I had found in the basement of my Grandpa Friedland's house. He'd been a horseman long before I was born, but by the time I came on the scene, his barn housed old furniture and my grandmother's green Buick. Regardless, the bridle was a treasure, and I would lovingly take apart the leather straps and condition it with Lexol, shining the silvery bit with steel wool until it gleamed. This horse hope chest containing all horse care supplies was my dream reservoir. It might be years and years before I got a horse, but deep down, I just knew one day my dream would come true.

CHAPTER 4

Prom Purge

I GOT ASKED to the prom when I was 15 by Steve, the dreamy bag boy. I worked as a checker at the mom-and-pop grocery store in our town, and met Steve when he skillfully arranged frozen foods and produce in brown paper bags for the customers who came through my line. He innocently kissed me goodnight on the front porch after our first date, which seemed like a very normal beginning to my dating career.

Steve was the wide receiver on his school's football team, and he had a cute round face with blond hair and blue eyes. He would have made a great Precious Moments figurine. Steve looked like the boy next door and almost was, as my parents knew his parents through small-town politics, and our older sisters had been friends in elementary school.

To make the prom dynamic more interesting, I ran the risk of being kicked out of my Baptist high school if the administration got wind of the fact I went to a dance. My small, ultra-conservative school believed dancing, rock music, and movies should be added to the list of the seven deadly sins. Because of prom, I was a good girl and a bad girl all at the same time.

Since Steve was something of a catch, I overlooked the fact we didn't really know each other well enough to go to the prom together. The extent of our communication prior to the, "Will you go to prom with me?" and me saying yes had only been along the lines of, "Steve, can you do a carryout?" or, "Will you exchange this carton of broken eggs?"

I thought it a little odd he asked me to the prom before we even had any sort of generic relationship established, let alone a dating relationship. I developed a theory as I got to know him better: he asked me to prom because he was rebounding.

Rumor had it (I heard this from the other bag boys at the store) Steve's girlfriend had dumped him abruptly. They had been together a long time. At age 16, I'm wondering how long the long time of that relationship was. Two months? Two weeks? My suspicion was Steve asked me out to save face. He had already purchased the prom tickets, so he had to do something with them. I was his Plan B.

Since Steve and I were not friends, only co-workers, and prom was about a month away, we began to date, meaning we went out on the three Friday nights leading up to the prom. The dates were lackluster, but gave me valid dating experience. The boy should pick you up and pay. You should spend lots of time in front of the mirror to ensure your hair and makeup look good. We went to a couple of movies and once to The Colonial for ice cream.

Setting up the date would go like this:

Steve would ask, "What do you want to do?"

"I don't care. What would you like to do?"

"Whatever it is you want to do."

At the movie theater:

Steve would ask, "Where do you want to sit?"

"It doesn't matter to me," I'd say.

"But where do you want to sit?"

"Anywhere."

It became evident after the first date the chemistry just wasn't there. However, I was committed. I had given him a Midwesterner yes and my mother had been lovingly sewing my one-shouldered royal blue dress from not one, but two patterns. I liked the top of a pattern from Butterick and the bottom from Vogue. The Vogue portion featured a fantastic, shimmering black-with-iridescent-blue-lace bustle. It was très chic chic!

The day of prom finally came. I had to grin and bear it, since it was evident Steve and I didn't even really have what it took to be friends. We didn't laugh together, he wasn't into horses, I wasn't into football. I felt sorry for him having to spend so much money on the event, and I felt sorry for myself having to go to a silly dance with a guy I didn't even like.

To Steve's credit, he was trying very hard to get the prom thing right, and borrowed his dad's flashy red Ford Taurus. When Steve picked me up my mom took pictures of us in our aqua blue living room. When we were done with our photo op, we went over to Steve's house so his parents could take our pictures. We smiled and posed, even though our hearts weren't into the prom or each other. The whole thing seemed forced.

Steve overestimated the time it would take to do pictures, so we were left with about an hour to kill prior to hopping into the Taurus and zooming away to the country club where the prom was taking place. Steve and I ended up watching Diff'rent Strokes with his parents. Gary Coleman was on the screen, Steve's parents were on the loveseat, Steve was in a tux with a royal blue cummerbund, and I was wearing a corsage.

During a commercial, Steve's mom approached me, photo-album in hand. "Here's a picture of Karen at prom."

"Oh, uh-huh. Nice." Karen, my sister's former classmate, was several years older than me. She went to prom in the '70s. I felt smug because she looked so *Brady Bunch* in her prom photo, and I looked so *Facts of Life* in real life.

I wasn't sure what to say when Steve's mom flipped from the prom photos to Karen's wedding photos smiling, "And here they are on their wedding day."

Karen MARRIED her prom date! Ew.

Good grief, I'm only 15, lady! My thoughts raced, but I forced a smile.

After a few more awkward moments of visiting with Steve's parents and finding out what Willis from the sitcom was talkin' 'bout, we left for the prom. What followed next made this day go down in infamy.

Green beans almondine and prime rib. Sounds tasty.

Was tasty. Until later on the dance floor when major stomach cramps hit. "I need to go use the bathroom. I'll be right back." I weaved past the other dancers pulsing in rhythm to Wham and sped out to the hallway, past the indoor waterfall and down the stairs to the ladies room. I made it there just in time. I ran into an empty stall and puked out my dinner.

I went to the sink to clean up, looked in the mirror and realized I had been healed. The cramps had fled, so I reapplied my lipstick and headed back to the dance floor.

I found Steve and we slow danced. We swayed cheek to cheek as he held me against his crisp tuxedo shirt. I couldn't decide if being near him was comfortable or weird. I had never been in such close proximity to a male who was not a family member before. And then my stomach twisted again.

"Steve, I've got to go to the bathroom again," I said as I separated from him darting to the restroom. I leaned over the first available toilet and another round of prime rib and green bean mush escaped into the bowl. I returned a second time to Steve and revealed I had been sick. "We can go if you want to," he offered.

Being a good martyr I vetoed his idea. "On no. I feel better now. We can stay." I was still trying to decide if slow dancing with a boy was my thing. I was determined to stick it out, food poisoning or not.

We stayed for another hour or two and I settled into a nice routine. I'd start to get a cramp, then I'd excuse myself and run to the bathroom, vomit and feel better so I'd go back and hit the dance floor with Steve again. At one point, I overheard some girls in the bathroom make a comment insinuating I had been drinking myself sick. I had not had a drop of alcohol, so those assumptions were way off.

We left the prom and went back to Steve's house, where we were going to round out our prom experience by watching some videos. I slipped into something a bit more comfortable—my best friend's borrowed oversize mauve Limited sweatshirt and black leggings. Steve cued up a movie about wolves. I sprawled out on the couch and was out like a light. The next thing I remember was waking up with another cramp in my side. I rushed to the bathroom and—shazam! I finally asked Steve to take me home.

Steve drove me to my house in silence. I got out of the Taurus and he walked with me to the front porch, the same porch where he kissed me on our first date only a few weeks prior. I looked at him with expectation and he said, "I hope you feel better."

"Sorry about tonight."

"Good bye."

I CONTINUED VOMITING and had terrible chills for the next 24 hours. I stayed in my bed curled up in the fetal position. My mom had to call Steve to tell him I couldn't go to Six Flags Great America amusement park, our post-prom activity. However, the day after the day after prom,

I was well again, and offered to take Steve riding with me. He agreed and we borrowed my parents' friend's horses I had been exercising for the previous few years.

I don't think Steve enjoyed the our trail ride through the green and golden fields trimmed with maples and oaks. I couldn't understand it. Even if the riding part was not his cup of tea, he should have been entranced by the scenery and company. I guess we were just too different.

The next time I went in to work at the grocery store, I heard from the other bag boys that Steve was telling everyone I had faked getting sick so I wouldn't have to kiss him at prom. That bothered me because it was untrue and felt like slander.

Steve and I never went out on another date. After prom, when Steve had to bag groceries for me we avoided direct eye contact. It was as if nothing had transpired between us.

"Steve, can you do a carry out for this customer?"

CHAPTER 5

Penny Sledding and the Horse Show

LONG BEFORE PROM, back in the days when I yearned for the horse of my dreams, I could still enjoy horses without having one. That principle of enjoyment minus commitment was clearly non-transferable to the dating realm.

When Gail, my best friend in elementary school, moved about 25 miles away to the country, little did I know her departure would pave the way for horse adventures. Her dad bought an apple farm, and the neighbors up the street had a palomino Quarter Horse named Penny. The sweet mare possessed a long, flaxen mane and tail that shimmered against her honey-toned coat. She could have been Mr. Ed's sister.

Gail and I used to ride Penny bareback and double, ambling through the clover between the rows of Jonathan and Golden Delicious trees. During fall when the apples were ready, we could even steer Penny right up under a branch and pluck the apples, eat them, and throw the cores over our shoulders to the ground in a trail behind us. The sweet crispness of those orchard apples were unparalleled by any supermarket's produce section. Walnut Hill Orchard was as close to Eden as I'll ever get.

Fun fact: In second grade Gail and I weighed the same, or at least that's what it said on our report cards—62 pounds. I'm still unclear as to why schools needed to report on a child's weight, and I dreaded the annual trip to the nurse's office to get weighed and measured. How embarrassing. What a way to set girls up for body image issues!

Unbeknownst to me, our body weight did not keep pace with each other as Gail and I grew over the next few years. This weight discrepancy led to a particularly painful situation one winter. Picture a bleak white landscape on a country road with two girls wearing bulky winter snowsuits. We resembled a fusion of sumo wrestlers and the Michelin Man.

Gail and I had the brilliant idea of taking each other sledding on the flat street—Penny our pal would provide the locomotion. We had a bridle, a clothesline and a sled. No sleigh. No saddle. No harness. Gail hopped on Penny and tied the rope around her waist. I tied the other end of the rope to the front of the sled. Gail kicked Penny and *voila!* I was sledding. Gail's house and the naked walnut trees lining her street blurred past as Penny walked on the side of the deserted road. It was almost as good as being in an actual horse drawn sleigh—like ones you see on Christmas cards.

We switched roles: Gail dismounted and I got up from the sled. I tied the rope around the waist of my snowsuit and Gail gave me a leg up onto Penny's wide back. I picked up the reins and Gail organized herself onto the sled.

"You ready?" She nodded. I gave the horse a slight nudge with the heel of my winter boot. Penny willingly moved forward; the sled stubbornly refused. It was partially stuck in the ditch on the side of the road. Like a cartoon, the horse stepped out from under me, my legs stayed in the shape of an inverted V, and then Shloop! Splat! I slammed into the icy ground hard—flat on my back and bottom.

I lay on the ground trying to breathe.

"Are you okay?" Gail came to my rescue, which might have been the driving force that launched her nursing career when she was all grown up. I was bruised but not broken.

There would be no more horse sledding. Bareback riding in the snow, yes. Horse sledding, no.

Gail and I had visions of Olympic greatness with access to Penny, our classy steed, and we decided it would be a good idea to enter her into a horse show. Nevermind neither of us had been in a horse show before. The only catch was Gail asked the Browns if we could take her to a show and they said no—something about not wanting to have Penny trailered somewhere.

Undeterred, Gail located a horse show at a stable within riding distance of her home and would require no trailering. She never followed up to ask if that would be okay. We both justified taking the initiative to ride Penny in the show because it was really no different from riding her around the fields and country roads which was her usual routine—and the Browns had no problem with the fields and road riding. Gail would ride her along the country road to the showgrounds, ride around in their field arena, and maybe take a few ribbons back on the return trip.

The whole week prior to the forbidden show, Penny was off in Missouri; her owners took her on trail riding vacation. This was terrible timing. Gail waited anxiously for Penny's return, and called me to tell me our show horse was not available.

"I went up to the pasture after school, and I didn't see her. Their trailer is still gone too. I'm worried they won't get back in time."

"Well, can't you go up to the house and ask when she'll be back?" I suggested.

"I can't. It would be too obvious; they'll know something's up. I never go to the door. We'll just have to wait."

Thankfully, the day before the horse show Penny returned from her excursion down south and celebrated her homecoming by rolling in a mud puddle. When Gail and I caught her at the crack of dawn on show day, Penny's golden coat was crusty brown. In order to transform Penny the trail horse into Penny, a correct English riding horse, we had a lot of work to do. We bathed her, cleaned her up, and realized her mane was all wrong. Too long.

"I think you need to make it shorter. That's how show horses' manes look in the books. Short," I offered.

Gail lopped off sections of white mane with household scissors. It shrank from 8 inches to about 4 in around five minutes. Truth be told, Penny's mane looked awful when we were done with it—like a little boy's bowl haircut. Next, we trimmed her muzzle whiskers with scissors. No more grandpa muzzle!

Gail got decked out in her riding attire for the 3-mile journey along Kishwaukee Valley Road to the show grounds. We gave Gail a bit of a head start to get to her destination and then Gail's dad drove me to the barn. Much to our dismay, when we arrived there were no trailers, no horses, no spectators and no concessions stands. The show had been canceled. No blue ribbons for us. No victory gallops around the arena. And now the damage to Penny's mane had been done for no real purpose.

To cover our misdeeds, once Gail had ridden the 3 miles back home and we took Penny to her field, we intentionally gathered cockleburrs and stuck them in her mane so it would disguise the length. The Browns would *never* know.

The Browns did find out about the show and they weren't happy. However, being good-hearted farm folk, they still allowed us the privilege to ride their horse. I never did find out what they thought the mane.

Life was so much simpler when borrowed horses were my world and boys were the furthest thing from my mind.

CHAPTER 6

Jim Dandy the Quarter Horse

ONE OF THE best things to happen to me as a child was when my dad ran for political office to represent several communities in the northwestern suburbs of Illinois. I experienced firsthand what was involved in our political process. I got to attend BBQ fundraisers and help fold and seal mailings. Politics is not nearly as glamorous nor as "dirty" as people may think—at least my involvement wasn't. I was a kid of 10.

The reason I say my dad's campaign was one of the best things that happened is because one of his supporters, a middle-aged lady named Cindy, found out I had an interest in horses. She owned and boarded about 10 horses on her property in the next town over and said I could come ride any time. Cindy became my riding patron, and my dad won the election.

The first time I went riding at Cindy's my older sister Linda accompanied me. As we drove away from our block of tidy ranch houses, we crossed the Fox River, which smelled terribly wormy after a fresh rain, and journeyed 3 miles to where the lot sizes grew larger and the homes followed suit.

When we arrived at Cindy's home, it seemed as though we were in a different country—England maybe. The front and back of her property contained horse pastures. To one side was a small lake, to the other, a grassy yard—the perfect size for a riding arena. Her property bordered a forest preserve that opened up to miles of riding trails and acres of prairie. It was paradise.

Cindy was zooming around on her John Deere tractor mowing the expansive lawn. When she saw us she stopped, greeted us and led the way to a small red shed in the middle of the pasture behind her house. It was the tack room. Inside, she grabbed three nylon halters with matching lead ropes. She passed off the red and green halters to my sister and me. "Follow me. Linda, you'll ride Peanut. Susan, you get Jim Dandy. I'll be riding Odessa."

We said okay and followed Cindy, hiking further back into her wooded field to find our horses. It was so exciting! I wondered what "my" horse would be like.

The horses were grazing leisurely in a grassy clearing. When they heard us approaching, they lifted their heads in unison and looked at us, still crunching their grassy mouthfuls. As we drew near they courteously turned toward us and allowed us to slide the halters on.

Jim Dandy was deep, dark red with a completely white face, slightly swayed back and a straggly tail. Peanut was golden-red, long and lean with a Roman nose and a white strip on his face. Odessa was a beautiful deep bay pony/horse. Depending on how long her hooves were, she could have passed for one or the other.

As I led Jim Dandy to the fence post by the red shed where I would groom him, he nuzzled me, on the lookout for a carrot or apple. He won me over at the first sniff.

Cindy never paid more than $500 for a horse, which even back in the 1980s was a pittance. Much like some of Hollywood's leading ladies, Cindy's horses never aged. Jim Dandy and Peanut remained 25 through the course of my junior high and high schools years. Although unlike a starlet, Jim Dandy detested cameras.

Linda and I tried a few different times to get pictures of ourselves on horseback. Jim Dandy would not stand still and pose nicely for the camera. He would back up or move sideways, anything to evade the perfect shot.

We curried and tacked the horses and were off on what was to become the first of many beautiful rides to come. I had the chance to take some horsemanship lessons at Camp Timber-Lee the summer before fourth grade, so I knew a bit more than the tips Jannee had given me on neck reining when I rode Mandy through our yard.

Cindy's horses were trained to be ridden English. This was quite a bit different. There was no saddle horn, but you got to use two hands on the reins instead of one. Instead of sitting to the bouncy trot, you got to post and alleviate a lot of jarring in your vertebrae.

In addition to my camp riding lessons, I had read at least a dozen books on horsemanship and had studied the black and white pictures of a rider sitting perfectly in the saddle. There was an imaginary vertical line from the top of the rider's head through the shoulder, elbow, hip, and heel.

I knew what textbook form should look like, and I noticed Cindy didn't look anything like the books' pictures. She was helmetless, with a cigarette dangling from her hand, hunched over like a jockey. Instead of enjoying the three gaits of walk, trot, and canter, Cindy limited her riding to two gaits. Fast and slower fast, with fast being her preference; it was a little scary. Cindy gave new meaning to the term hell bent for leather.

Looking back, I'm not sure how Cindy managed to keep her fingernails so long and red and fashionable working around the horses and taking care of her land. She did all the mowing on the John Deere and all the feeding. Wrestling with bales of hay half her size and grooming and tacking up the horses—all with a cigarette teetering precariously off her lips.

One time when I went riding in the middle of winter, Cindy chased down snowmobilers. She took off at a mad gallop—they weren't supposed to be on the Illinois Prairie Path—only bikes, walkers, and horses allowed. She really gave them a piece of her mind—if they could hear her over the drone of their powerful engines.

Even though I eventually got to ride Odessa and Peanut, over time Jim Dandy unofficially became "my" horse. I'm not sure how that evolved, but we were a pair. I'd ride him bareback with a halter. I'd feed him carrots, joyfully groom him for hours and take apart every piece of his bridle and saddle and oil them to keep them in good shape.

As I became more of a regular out at Cindy's place, I made friends with a cluster of equally horse-crazy girls who boarded their horses in the big pasture. In the summer, every day held new riding adventures. There were trails to be explored, jumps to be sailed over, and wild raspberries to be eaten.

One lazy summer day, we rode over to the cemetery in front of Cindy's property. The lawn was well manicured and the footing even. It just begged to be trotted and cantered on. We even used some of the lower headstones as jumps. Looking back, I see that's probably not the most respectful way to conduct oneself in a graveyard, but our impulsive actions were in essence a celebration of life—isn't that the reason cemeteries exist anyway?

A few times we rode the horses bareback to a swimming hole. I had seen the movie *The Black Stallion* and knew horses could swim. I remember the underwater shots showing The Black's sleek legs paddling in the ocean.

In July and we donned our swimsuits and a few of my horse comrades and I took a ride in a new direction. Instead of going through the forest preserve, we rode alongside Dunham Road for a couple of miles and then turned down a narrow wooded road and found a bridle path along the side.

The homes we passed were the stuff of which fairytales were made. Two-story colonial houses rose up regally from their perfectly manicured lawns set far back from the road. Several of them had small barns off to the side that looked like miniature versions of the houses.

Riding arenas with white painted jumps graced several of the properties. I knew Wayne, Illinois was what heaven must be like, except for the mosquitoes and horseflies that came out in droves in the middle of summer.

We crossed the edge of someone's property line to another path leading to a grove of maples and oaks, which gave way to a small pond. It was totally secluded and just waiting for us to swim in. I hung back, observing my three riding companions beeline for the water. Their horses willingly plunged into the quarry and the girls giggled and shrieked as they swam around, feminine centaurs birthed in rural Illinois. It looked so fun and I followed. Jim Dandy goodnaturedly joined in the frolicking.

When he was in deep enough the water covered his back, my legs slid out behind me and I grabbed his chestnut neck in a bear hug. Holding on to the reins was unnecessary; I wasn't really in control and soaked leather is tremendously slippery. The reins would have slid through my hands anyway.

Just as I was getting the hang of this new way of riding/swimming, my horse's head disappeared into the water. By the time my brain processed what I was sure was ensuing danger, the crimson head and neck rose straight from the depths and a spray of pond liquid spewed out of his flared nostrils. This beast I had known and loved as a horse seemed part whale, part marine dinosaur. It was such a mystery that Jim Dandy was seemingly comfortable in the water and such a strong swimmer. I couldn't imagine he had been in a swimming hole before. How did he do it?

"Watch out!" someone yelled. "Look at the floaties!" Drifting dangerously close to me was a cluster of fresh horse apples. I didn't know whose horse had pooped in the pond, but it was evident Jim and I needed to flee. As I pulled the rein to the right to evade the greenish brown grenades, I heard, "Eeeww! Look!" and more laughter. Jim Dandy had lifted his tail and let loose his own projectiles. By the end of our time in the water, all the horses had pooped, depositing manure flotillas along the way. The four of us were successful in swimming out of the way of the bounty by lifting our legs out of the water and perching on the horses in a squat whenever a brown bomb came too close for comfort.

When we grew tired of the pond, our teen riding party turned to head home. All the fly spray had worn off and the horses' tails worked overtime swishing left and right. They intermittently shook their long necks to shoo away the insect pests. We must have been a sight to behold: soaked hair, swimsuit-clad, trotting along the road on our black, bay, and chestnut horses. It was supremely fun, but not at all glamorous, no matter what the advertisements in women's magazines try to depict with skinny models on horseback.

PART II

Novice Rider, Novice Dater

CHAPTER 7

Daytona's Derby Bid

THE REASON I began working my first job as a cashier at the minimum acceptable worker's permit age of 14 was so I could save enough money to buy a horse. Going to prom with the bag boy was not even on my radar when I filled out the job application. My horse hope chest was full, but my savings account was not.

My parents had made it clear through the years we didn't have the money for a horse. They explained buying a horse, although expensive, was not the financial concern. It was the upkeep that made it cost prohibitive—the grain and hay, horseshoes and vet visits. My two older sisters were in college, and on top of that, my parents had a tuition bill for my private school. And so I determined if my parents couldn't buy a horse for me, I'd just have to do it myself.

Once I started my job, I greeted every payday with a smile. I would proudly take my check to Home Federal Savings and Loan, where I would slide the deposit slip next inside the brown savings register and hand it over to the teller. Like a squirrel, I was storing away for the future.

Even though I still had the privilege of getting to ride our family friend Cindy's horses whenever I wanted to, I felt like a pest every time I called her to ask permission to ride. She never once said no. As much as I loved Jim Dandy, the ancient foxhunter, I still wanted a horse of my own. Borrowing horses could never be as fulfilling as ownership.

After scraping together $1,500 from allowances, collecting aluminum cans, birthday money and my job at the store, I was ready to enter into the world of horse ownership! And my parents finally said yes.

I knew it was going to be hard work. I knew it was going to be expensive. I knew you should never buy a young horse as a first horse. Yet I disregarded that common sense rule I had read in scores of horse books from both the 636 Horse Husbandry and 798 Equestrian Sports Dewey Decimal Systems sections of the library. This was before the Internet.

They say love is blind. They say you lose your senses. I can attest to that. Daytona, the 3-year-old registered Quarter Horse gelding I met through an ad in the *Daily Courier News,* charmed me and I lost my senses.

My mom and I drove about ten miles west of town, past corn and soybean fields, out into the country to see if this horse could be the one. I saw him grazing in the pasture as our car pulled into the driveway. He looked so at ease. Head down, happily munching—an orange dot on a green background. The owner caught him and led him over to us. His ears swiveled forward and he seemed agreeable. "Would you like me to saddle him up and you can take him for a spin?" his owner asked.

I assented and offered to help. I always liked to check

the girth when other people saddled a horse for me. I was scarred by my sister Renee's attempts to tighten a western cinch on another friend's family horse one time. My ride started out great but midway through I was riding the horse from under his belly.

We groomed and tacked up Daytona and then I mounted onto his comfortably wide back.

"You can just ride him in the front pasture." The moment I settled in the saddle, I knew I had to have him. He was pretty, in my price range, the breed I wanted, and had good brakes. The reason he was so willing to whoa wasn't solely because he was responsive to my riding aids. It was because Daytona was one of *the* laziest horses on the planet, which I found out the extent of later.

I rode the perimeter of the pasture at a walk to get a feel for him. Then we trotted. It was slow and smooth. I honestly don't remember if I cantered or not. I was already stuck on this horse, and I didn't want to lose him.

A few months earlier I had fallen in love with a young, black mare named CC, and my love was spurned. I test rode her and was dazzled. I called the owner to tell her I wanted to buy CC, and she said someone else was going to buy her. I didn't believe her. Deep down I had this sixth sense the owner didn't want me to have her because I'd never owned a horse.

After that rejection phone call, I took the hot rollers out of our pink bathroom and threw them into the hallway. I cried and carried on about how unfair life was. My dad tried to comfort me with a sports analogy, explaining how Pete Rose, a.k.a. Charlie Hustle, never gave up; he always persevered. (This was long before Pete was indicted for gambling.)

I couldn't let this horse I had fallen for in record time get away from me like CC had. I hoped Daytona's owner liked me. I dismounted and told her I really liked him, but I had to think it over and I would call her.

Later that afternoon I phoned the seller. "I want to buy him. I'm wondering if I could pay you $1,100?" His owner was asking $1,200. I was unskilled in the ways of negotiation.

She accepted my offer! We discussed details and set up a day to have Daytona trailered over to Cindy's. I went to the bank and got a cashier's check. I gathered my supplies from the horse hope chest and took them out to Cindy's red shed serving as a tack room and set up shop. I bought a brand new green halter and lead rope I knew would contrast beautifully with Daytona's chestnut coat.

The girls I had ridden with a few years earlier had moved on to boys, so I was the lone boarder. Cindy needed help in keeping her pastures "mowed." With his appetite, Daytona did not disappoint.

The day I had dreamed of all my life had arrived! Daytona, my first horse, the culmination of my dreams was delivered. The trailer drove up the hill of the long pebbled driveway. The seller's husband got out and I handed him the cashier's check. He opened the latch on the back door of the trailer and then unhooked the butt bar. He went inside and unsnapped Daytona's halter from the trailer's hook and led him slowly backward, down the ramp. Daytona scudded down, head held high. He stood at the back of the trailer, ears alert, head turning to survey his new surroundings. He let out a loud whinny and I walked over to take the lead rope. He was magnificent and he was mine!

CHAPTER 8

Spicy Valentine

WHEN I WASN'T out with Daytona or working at the grocery store to support him, I was dreaming about my crush: Grant Rollins. My pittery pattery feelings for him began in sixth grade when I first attended a small, private Christian school. Grant's sense of humor, blue eyes, and preppy style drew me in like ants to a picnic. I liked this boy so intensely I barely spoke to him, although I was friends enough with him that on the last day of school, I'd have him sign my yearbook. I would read his, "Susan, you're cool. Have a fun summer and stay out of trouble. Grant" over and over trying to interpret exactly what he meant and determine if perhaps he too had an unspoken crush on me.

My heart shifted a bit during my junior year when I had speech class with Grant's older brother. I soon developed a crush on him that dwarfed my previous crush. Ryan earned primary crush status and Grant fell to secondary crush. There were some good genes in that family.

Ryan, a star player on the soccer team, looked a bit like Tom Cruise as Maverick in his *Top Gun* glory. Ryan was articulate and confident. In a word—hot. I liked Ryan so much I wouldn't speak to him. I couldn't speak to him, even though we were classmates, ironically, in a speech class with a dozen students. This venue was perfect for getting to know one another, and we had a vibrant teacher, a recent college graduate who made our lessons engaging.

One day she gave us a new seating chart, and I was assigned a desk right next to Ryan! I kept my eyes straight ahead, focusing on the board. Ryan was friendly and tried to make small talk, but I was too overwhelmed by his presence to respond. Every day I languished by his side.

Instead of prom, which was considered by our ultra-conservative school as "worldly," our school had a Valentine's Banquet. It was the big dating event of the year, although officially, our school handbook said it neither encouraged nor discouraged dating. The Valentine's Banquet was just like prom without the dancing, dresses that showed skin, rock music, and physical contact. After the meal in place of the dancing there was special music which means someone sings a hymn while another person plays the piano, and to wind the evening down nicely, a youth pastor preached. It's so obvious why everyone clamored to go.

One day junior year during the bus ride home, my friend Rachael had a smug look on her face. "I know *someone* who's going to ask *you* to the Valentine's Banquet," she gushed.

"Stop joking, Rachael. I'm not going. Nobody's going to ask me."

The Valentine's Banquet was for the really pretty and popular girls—the ones who had actual boyfriends, not a horse as a boyfriend. Not for girls like me who worked at a grocery store to pay for hay.

"Seriously. I know someone who wants to go with you, and he's going to ask you." She smirked, enjoying her status of being privy to a secret.

My mind instantly went to the guys in my class I would least enjoy being on a date with. I hoped it wasn't Palmer. He idolized Donald Trump and came to class with a briefcase and a newspaper. He picked his nose and was rumored to put mustard on every food item for lunch.

Then there was Brett. He was kind of my friend, but he was really weird. He was part of the popular guy group because he would be their jester. They all liked him, but they all made fun of him, and he didn't mind. He relished the attention. He spoke fast without articulating syllables, and there seemed to always be small milky strings of spit at the corners of his mouth. Neither classmate would be my dream date, so it probably was one of them.

"Who?!? Rachael! You have to tell me!" I was in agony.

"Okay. But promise when he asks, you'll act like you didn't know."

I promised and waited.

"It's Ryan!" she proclaimed after a dramatic pause.

"Stop it, Rachael. That's not funny!"

"No, I'm serious. I talked to him and he asked me for your phone number. He wants to go with you!"

How could this be possible? Ryan?! Gorgeous Ryan. Soccer-playing, Polo wearing, Tom Cruise-lookalike Ryan?

"He really asked for my number?"

"Yes! He's going to call you soon and ask you to the banquet."

Rachael's bus ride revelation changed my life. At least for a couple weeks. It still didn't change my interaction with Ryan. I made sure to definitely NOT look his way or go out of my way to talk to him in class. I knew his secret and had to act cool—let him come to me.

Even though I had to go lowkey on the outside, on the inside I was ecstatic, and my focus became the banquet. I went home and told my mom I needed to go shopping for a dress. This was going to be way more exciting than prom. This time I *wanted* to be with my date.

After a couple of trips to different shopping malls, I found the perfect dress—a red satin number from Talbots. (Where else could you get a nice dress at least knee-length without a slit and a neckline no more plunging than the allowable horizontal hand's width if you placed your index finger over your sternum?) It had short sleeves and a pleated waist and was very matronly—it would pass the stringent dress code, and I loved it.

As soon as my mom and I burst through the door, dress in hand, I asked my dad if there were any calls for me. Nope.

There was no call from Ryan that night or the next, or the one following, and Ryan didn't try to get a chance to talk to me alone at school. The banquet was only a week away. I was worried.

I was embarrassed to bring up the subject with my in-the-know friend, but thought maybe reviewing the facts would provide a clue as to what was going on with Ryan. And so on another bus ride home I questioned her.

"Rachael, Ryan hasn't called, and I don't think he's going to. Are you sure he said he was going to ask me?"

"Yes. I'm positive. I gave him your number."

"Do you think he lost it? Should I say something to him?"

"I wouldn't. I'll see what I can find out."

"Thanks," I tried to respond optimistically, but I knew that it was too good to be true. A cute, smart, funny, popular guy like Ryan would never ask a tall, shy, bookworm horse girl like me to the banquet. It was hopeless.

The next night he called! I picked up the marigold receiver in our kitchen, stunned.

"Hi, this is Ryan, is Susan there?"

"This is she," I responded in a professional voice.

"Hi Susan. I'm calling because I know you heard from a little bird I was going to ask you to the Valentine's banquet."

So it *was* true!

"Well, that was my intention but I realized I have another engagement that night. But, I would still like to take you out . . ."

Disappointment quickly chased away my elation. I was talking to Ryan—he called me!—yet he was telling me he wasn't going to take me to the Valentine's Banquet. He called to not invite me to the banquet. Of course. I knew it was too good to be true!

I felt like the biggest fool. I had seen this in a *Brady Bunch* episode—the one where "something suddenly came up." I was skeptical of the other "engagement," and failed to show enthusiasm for the "would still like to take you out" part. It was as though he didn't even say those hopeful words. I mumbled some kind of response and hung up.

To make matters worse, a few days later in speech I had to do a pantomime in front of the class. Yes, a pantomime in which one doesn't speak at all in a public speaking class! The scenario I had to act out was "Waiting for a Late Date." Mortified at the dating theme and prospect of performing clownish motions with Ryan dead center in the audience, I flailed.

After pacing around in the front of the classroom, anxiously looking at my nonexistent watch on my left wrist and "fixing" my hair and makeup in an imaginary mirror for a few minutes, I had to let loose with the climax of my Marcel Marceau performance.

I pretended to hear a knock, and purposefully walked over to the front and center of the classroom—the spot that was supposed to be my front door. Reaching for the door knob, I opened it wide and seized a ghost box of chocolates and flowers. I looked at them and then threw them in the face of the "date." I pictured Ryan's face on the other side of the threshold—because he was actually in my line of vision when looking out into the class. Slamming the nonexistent door shut as if to say, "Take that!" I slapped and slid my hands together to triumphantly wash my hands of the situation—of the pantomime itself and of Ryan and the non-date.

I power walked back to my desk with my eyes focused on the carpeting. The room's silence allowed the critical little voice in my head to jeer my shadow boxing performance. My teacher sat in the last row of desks, quietly jotting down feedback. I was relieved the pantomime was over, but was silently shriveling up in my seat from the embarrassment.

My friend Julian leaned across his desk and whispered, "What were you doing up there?" I learned from him later, according the audience's perspective, instead of looking like an impatient girl waiting on a late date, I looked like a marionette jerking around, pacing and throwing a temper tantrum.

Later my teacher handed me a piece of paper where a large C- glared at me with several comments explaining how I could have improved my presentation. As if my life weren't miserable enough, my mom and I had to return the modest red dress intended for the banquet to Talbot's.

About a week later, February 14 arrived, and with it the annual Valentine cookie delivery during lunch. It was a class fundraiser. You could buy a heart cookie and have a customized message delivered to a friend or "lover." I got a cookie that said, "Spicy Mama." It was sent anonymously, but I found out from Rachael's younger brother Patrick it was from Ryan.

Patrick was a year behind me in school and also a classmate in speech. Patrick revealed Ryan felt bad about the whole Valentine's banquet uninvitation and told me the whole story. It turned out someone else wanted to ask me to the banquet—someone who was Ryan's friend. Someone who *really* liked me. And had liked me for a long time.

"Are you kidding? Who is it?" I asked.

"Brett."

Brett the jester with the stringy spit mouth.

Why Brett? I didn't like him that way. I couldn't take him seriously, and he wasn't even cute. Or cool. Or preppy. And what was bewildering was Brett didn't even end up asking me. Patrick said Ryan was mad at Brett since he bowed out so Brett could ask me, but then Brett chickened out. I felt like such a fool, although it was a relief to know Ryan's intentions were good, even though my lack of encouragement when he called to explain why he didn't follow through to ask me out probably shot down any prospect of going on a date with this boy.

The rest of the school year passed without incident. Neither Ryan nor Brett asked me out.

I continued to pine for Ryan and treasured the hour every day when we'd share the same row in speech class, even though I never spoke to him again. At least not until the last week of school when I asked him to sign my yearbook.

CHAPTER 9

Daytona's New Digs

AS OFTEN HAPPENS with first loves, my dream horse turned into a nightmare. I was duped by his smooth gaits, friendly demeanor and the ease of getting him to halt. I was not prepared for two grievous vices. He didn't start out with them, but developed them shortly after I took ownership. Daytona pulled when led with a halter, and he bucked when I cued him to canter. Daytona was a handful, and I was in over my head as a first-time horse owner.

All the books say to get an older, seasoned, sane horse if you're a new owner, a horse with one foot in the grave. I figured I was the exception to that rule. After all, I had been riding for about five years if you counted my first ride on Mandy in our yard, and I'd gone to horse camp and had taken lessons here and there. I hadn't ridden consistently for five years, but five years sounded like a long time.

I deluded myself into thinking I was an experienced horse person since I had read every book from the library and subscribed to both *Practical Horseman* and *Horse-play*.

Daytona's pulling grew serious. My hands and fingers frequently were rubbed with moist, open rope burns from desperately trying to hang on to the nylon lead rope when Daytona went after a mouthful of grass. I sometimes felt like he was capable of running me over. In a collision of a 1,200 pound horse and a 120 pound person, I knew who would win.

The bucking was scary and somewhat predictable. I would be riding along, enjoying the scenery and would give the cue to canter. Daytona would forcefully drop his head and neck all the way to his knees, while at the same time launching his hindquarters off the ground. The head jerk alone would pull me out of the saddle and up onto his neck. The additional propulsion of his back end was capable of landing my back end on the ground. He was successful a few times.

How could my wonderful horse could have such an evil side? I started dreading going for a ride. This was not how my horse dream was supposed to play out. I began to wonder if it was the kelp feed supplement I had given him that was making him kooky.

My horse lover's honeymoon was definitely over.

In less than a year of horse ownership, I wondered what I had gotten myself into with this horse that infuriated me, scared me and provoked me to tears. I wished Jim Dandy, the borrowed horse I used to ride was still alive, but age had finally won out. He was wizened and hard-mouthed, but at least he didn't have a split personality. I never felt like he was intentionally trying to plant me onto the ground.

To make matters worse, I had no one to help me with my horse since he was boarded in our friend's backyard. I was alone in my dysfunctional relationship.

My salvation came one day while my mom was at the beauty shop. I guess she was pouring out her concerns over my safety and her helplessness because she didn't know anything about horses, when her hairdresser suggested my mom should talk to a woman named Sheri who worked a couple of chairs over. Sheri had horses in her backyard; she bred and trained Appaloosas.

After a quick conversation, Sheri gave my mom her number and said I should call her. Soon after that phone call she came over to visit Daytona in his pasture paradise. After observing my normal routine of catching, grooming, tacking, and riding, Sheri said she thought she could help me.

Sheri was soft spoken, and I learned later not only cut hair, but worked at a frame store at the mall, went to art classes, had two teenage kids *and* took care of all six of her horses. She mucked the stalls, fed, and turned them out every day. She had toned arms for a mom—there was no dangly flab on her triceps.

She explained to me part of Daytona's problem was his life didn't have any structure or discipline. It was great he lived in such a natural environment out on several acres like a wild Mustang, but he was starting to think he *was* a wild Mustang. He needed a routine and a job. "I have an extra stall. If you moved him to my house, I could help you train him."

I didn't want to leave Cindy's because she had been a kind horse patron, letting me ride her horses whenever I wanted to. And the location with the forest preserve trails was idyllic. Yet I knew I had to move him because what good were idyllic fields if I was too nervous to ride through them for fear my horse was going to toss me off and go galloping away?

And so we moved. Daytona settled into his new, more structured environment. He was in a stall at night and turned out with one or two other horses in different smaller fields during the day. Sheri would dispense wisdom to me as she worked over the stalls, fishing out the damp and soiled shavings into her wheelbarrow. I hung on to her every word.

"Have you tried leading him with a chain and backing him up if he walks ahead of you?"

"No. I've seen people use a chain on a halter, but I don't know how. I don't have one. And isn't it kind of mean? I don't want to hurt him."

"I don't think you're going to hurt Daytona. He's a very strong horse. The chain just serves as a little reminder to him you're there and he needs to listen to you. You won't pull on it long. Just a tiny jerk. I'll show you when I'm done with these stalls."

She suggested I get involved in 4-H. Her daughter who was a few years younger than me was in it, and I could tag along with her and make some new friends and learn more about horses.

4-H is a lovely organization with dedicated people who try to help kids learn animal husbandry. I did well in extracurricular activities like horse judging, a competition in which kids get to judge the conformation of four horses and then give oral reasons for placing them the way they did. You'd see if your placement matched up with what the real horse judge thought. If so, you'd get points. I was not a star member in other respects. I got a white ribbon for my strawberry-filled turnover, and the one fair I took Daytona to was not exactly stellar.

In the middle of the halter class, in which the rider leads the horse around as he's judged on conformation and appearance, my horse spread his back legs, let it all hang out (quite literally) and peed smackdab in the middle of the show ring. He personally contributed to watering down the arena, perhaps in an attempt to keep it dust-free. Or just to show off. I was mortified. I surmised Daytona was trying to garner attention, "Watch THIS, Judge! Look at me!"

After that display as we were lined up head to tail, Daytona somehow kept inching closer to the horse's butt in front of us. I was decked out in my English riding habit and hoping I looked very upper class. Daytona's butt sniffing wasn't helping my act.

I subtly tried to pull his reins back to get his head away from our neighbor. Daytona persisted in his antics and jerked his head right into the black tail of the horse in front of us. The horse squealed. Daytona jumped back and the reins flew out of my hand and somehow temporarily laced around the tail of the accosted horse. I quickly picked up the reins as they fell out of the tail onto the dust of the arena and tried to act nonchalant. I don't think I fooled anyone.

CHAPTER 10

King Kong

I WENT ON a few dates here and there during college, but nothing notable enough to chronicle since horses and studying dominated my existence. I had a sense Daytona and I were going in different directions in life, and it would soon be time to move on. It wasn't him, it was me.

My equestrian aspirations were ascending and Daytona was not complying. He found it easier and more amusing, I'm sure, to run and crash through a jump than to actually pick up his feet, fold his knees, and sail over it.

This realization unfolded my junior year when I found an equally horse-loving friend in one of my political science classes who teamed up with me to found the Wheaton College Equestrian Team. We had discovered old yearbooks from the 1920s and 1930s that showed Wheaton students riding, as it was often a helpful skill for those who became missionaries in remote parts of the world. We had less spiritual ambitions with our riding.

Around this time I had a regular babysitting job in the same horsey town where I first learned to ride on Jim

Dandy, the bald-faced Quarter Horse. The family told me one of their neighbors was a horse trainer, and I should meet her because she was really nice and I'd like her. They were right.

Joanne, a hunter/jumper trainer, was warm and cheerful. There was not an introverted bone in her body, and she would talk the entire lesson long.

"Do you know how narrow his spine is? You need to ride evenly on both sides."

"When you come up this line you have to be straight. Imagine a ditch on both sides filled with lions and tigers—you can't fall in."

After a handful of lessons on her horses, I asked her come out to meet Daytona, and a few weeks later I moved him to the barn where she was training so we could grow our skills.

The new boarding stable inhabited former farmland; paddocks and grand pastures stretched across scores of acres like a miniature Lexington, Kentucky. A big red and white barn stood in the middle of the verdant backdrop at the end of a long, gravel driveway. It was there I met King Kong.

I first noticed Kong, as we affectionately called the chestnut gentle giant, shuttling various little girls around the arena. The girls' jodhpur-clad, stick legs barely reached halfway down Kong's sides.

Kong was a towering 17-hand, 3-inch Appendix Quarter Horse gelding. Translated into layman's terms, he was 5 feet 8 inches meaning if I stood next to him, he was so tall I couldn't see over his back. There was pretty much no way of mounting without something or someone to stand on. He stood out in the crowd much like an NBA star walking through an airport, like the time I spotted Kareem Abdul-Jabbar at LAX.

"Turn left and point him to the center of the fence," Joanne shouted from underneath her white baseball cap. Her signature look was the cap, black leggings, baggy T-shirt and Lee Press on nails—in red. Kong was Joanne's horse.

There was a schooling show at my new barn, and practice jumps were set up on the side lawn. My target was the center of the two white jump standards, a small X made of two rails, about 18 inches high in the middle. Joanne told me to sit still and grab mane and Kong would do all the work.

I pointed the giant toward the fence and the propulsion of Kong's movement lightly jolted my upper body forward, where I momentarily hovered over the top of his neckline, hands pressing into into his neck so I would stay balanced mid flight. We landed and I stopped him a few strides away and turned around to face it from the other side. I smiled.

Joanne raised a pole, making the fence straight across. The jump was still small so I didn't give it a second thought and trotted toward the center. Soon, Joanne coached me to keep jumping the fence back and forth, first from one direction and then from the other direction. As I practiced my straight line halt a few strides out from landing after the fence, she would sneak up and raise the fence again and again. When it got to about three and a half feet, my nerves were rattling and my pulse rising.

"He could walk over this in his sleep," Joanne insisted. "All you have to do is look beyond it and breathe." Easier said than done. Joanne assured me a second time stating Kong was so big and well-trained he could jump that size fence from a standstill. I nodded.

My heart was racing, but I did what she instructed me to do. I had never jumped a fence that high, let alone on a horse I had never ridden before!

King Kong's powerful strides propelled us toward the seemingly massive fence. We got closer, closer and then the giant chestnut lurched forward and we were airborne for a brief second. He landed, front feet, then hind feet. We cleared the fence cleanly, took a few more canter strides away from the barn toward the green fields, and then my new friend began to slow and halted as I squeezed the reins and sat taller in the saddle.

I smiled as I turned toward Joanne. She chirped out congratulations and encouragement. It was a thrill— thundering toward and sailing over a formidable obstacle in perfect harmony with a magnificent creature. Through that experience and countless similar jumping sessions, I slowly learned the irony of equitation: riding best by doing the least. The way to be a great rider was to be balanced and breathe.

I patted King Kong on his damp auburn neck and my affection for him took root. Little did I know in spite of my current horse relationship with Daytona, Kong and I had a future together. Here's how that partnership began.

The summer after I graduated from college, I traveled

to Spain for six weeks *para aprender Español*, and I leased Daytona to a woman who wanted a nice, quiet horse to ride for a few months. Even though I was in a dreamy foreign land on the Mediterranean, my horse ended up having a summer romance. The woman who leased Daytona fell in love with him and wanted to be with him forever.

It was sad to think of selling my first horse, my diamond in the rough. However, Joanne informed me she had known the woman a long time, and her previous horse was a Thoroughbred mare she owned for 18 years. When the mare died, the woman had it buried in a pet cemetery. Daytona would be going to a good home.

I moved forward and sold him for $1,500. I made a $400 "profit" and gained a wealth of experiences that made me a better horsewoman.

Although I was horseless for the first time in several years, it seemed the world was opening up for me in the form of riding other people's horses. Daytona and I had come to the end of what we could teach each other and it was time to move on.

How is it horsekeeping so resembles dating?

CHAPTER 11

Just Desserts?

"I THINK YOU should just tell me what we're doing and where you guys are taking us," I urged Eric as we sat in the back row of the church van. I was in my mid-twenties and no longer as shy as I had been as a teen.

"Can't do that," he said shaking his head.

"Come on. Just give me one little hint. I won't say anything to Sandra and Pam. I promise." Sandra and Pam were sitting with their "dates" in the front and second rows of the van.

It was October, and about a week earlier I'd been sick with the flu, on my couch in my small, 60s-vibe apartment (complete with pink refrigerator) I rented from my Grandma.

My phone rang; it was Sandra, my women's small-group leader from church. She sounded excited and wanted to come over right then and drop something off for me. I told her I was really sick and did not want to transmit germs. She promised she wouldn't stay long, just drop off the item and be on her way.

A short while later, Sandra burst into my home with a gleam in her eye. "I have a formal invitation for you from the guys." She handed me a homemade blue card with a white piece of fabric, a ship's sail in the center.

"They made it themselves. Cute, huh."

"What guys?" It was kind of a surprise to hear I made the invite list for a group date. All those hours at the barn did not lend themselves well to me meeting eligible bachelors.

"Oh, you know, some guys from church—Eric, Dan, and Mike. Here, read it. Pam and I got one too."

On the back of the sailboat card was a message indicating the guys requested the honor of my presence for a special event the following Saturday night. The group date would commence at Sandra's house at 6 p.m. I would need to wear something nice, but bring along a change of clothes—clothes it would be okay if they got dirty.

"You're going, right?" she said in a tone indicating I had to go, regardless of what I might have planned or my state of health.

I said okay, but quickly added if I was still sick, I'd have to cancel.

"You'll be fine, silly. It's a week away."

I tried to pry out of her what the mystery date was all about. What we would be doing, where we'd be going. I wasn't really close friends with the three guys.

"Come on. It'll be fun!" Sandra reassured me the guys wanted to get to know us better, and they wanted to take us out for an old-fashioned good time.

The night of the group date arrived and we met at Sandra's home. About five minutes later an extra long burgundy church van pulled up into the driveway. This was our limo for the evening. The three eligible bachelors piled out and greeted us warmly.

"Okay, ladies. Are you ready for an adventure?" Dan asked. He worked at the church and pulled strings to procure the van so we could all ride together. We nodded and climbed into the sweet ride with the oversized church logo of a tree by a river. We were going to have some holy fun.

I sat in the way back section, which turned out great because I wound up next to Eric. He and I were a little beyond the acquaintance level of friendship, and conversation was easy. Getting him to tell the secret was not.

From the driver's seat Dan announced, "For Phase I we're going to take you to dinner—hope you're hungry. And we're treating. The place we're going is a favorite of mine."

About 30 minutes later, we pulled into the parking lot of a restaurant in the middle of a strip mall. The place was cozily dark and very crowded. Our party had reservations. The guys had everything planned. Impressive.

The three of us "couples"—I tried to figure out who I was supposed to be paired with, but I think it was meant to be vague—sat at a round table and spent the time at the restaurant in intentional, "get-to-know you" conversation. We talked about where we went to school, where we grew up, how long we had been attending our church.

We discussed movies and Seinfeld episodes. The lively spirit around the table and the meals were delicious.

Once we finished our entrees, the server asked if we'd be interested in looking at the dessert menu. Dan spoke for us, saying we'd be having dessert during Phase II. Truer words were never spoken.

My badgering did nothing to convince Eric to tell me what on earth the guys had planned for Phase II. I grew very apprehensive as we headed further away from the suburbs and ended up driving down a dark, wooded country road. I don't watch horror movies, but I felt certain our surroundings could have been a setting for one.

"Are you sure you can't tell me? I'm very good at keeping secrets," I pleaded.

"Sorry," Eric said with a grin.

"Come on. Pleeease?"

He was a stone wall.

The van turned down a narrow driveway, and from the driver's seat Dan announced, "Here we are. This is the house I grew up in. My sister lives here now." He parked the car in front of the rambling farmhouse.

The chilly autumnal air, the black sky, and the dense trees surrounding the property made me think the boys were up to no good. Were they going to take us on a "hike" into the woods and then desert us and then sneak up on us and scare us by jumping out from behind the trees? Did they make a haunted house out of the barn? Whatever the guys had planned was not on the up and up, despite their saintly mode of transportation.

I made a decision if they told us we were going to go walking in the woods I would abstain, citing my recent flu as reason to not be out in the cold.

"Okay, ladies. Get your change of clothes. Let's go in." Pam, Sandra, and I grabbed our bags and exchanged puzzled glances.

All six of us stepped into the house and were greeted by Dan's sister. She led us girls to a spare bedroom where we were instructed to change into our clothes that could get dirty. The tension in the room was thick. I was a wreck.

"If they take us into the woods and try to sneak up on us, I'm going to be really mad," I asserted.

"I know. What are they doing? Why do we need to wear old clothes?" Sandra wondered aloud.

"I kept trying to get it out of Eric when we were in the van. He wouldn't say a word. They're up to something, and it's *not* good."

When the three of us had changed, we met up with the grinning guys in the kitchen.

"Okay, so what are we doing, Dan?" Sandra questioned with a not-amused smile on her face.

"You'll see. Be patient."

Mike and Eric and Dan had a sinister air about them.

"You know, I just got over the flu and if you guys are going outside, I should probably stay here. I'm still not 100 percent," I tried to sound composed and casual.

"Oh, you'll be fine. We'll actually be inside," Dan assured.

We'll be inside? How was that possible? What in the

world was going on? Why did we need "clothes that can get dirty" inside?

Dan urged us forward and we followed him out the front door like lambs to the slaughter. I hated the situation. I kept trying to read Eric's smug expression but couldn't discern anything.

All three of us "couples" walked the short distance to the old white barn.

Crap! I thought. *I knew it! They made a haunted house.*

I hate haunted houses. I even get a little creeped out by the benign one at Disneyland. I tried to keep a poker face so they wouldn't know I was scared.

"Here we are, ladies." Dan paused in front of the sliding barn door, while Mike and Eric stood near the two handles ready to slide their doors open.

"Behind these doors there is a game we have prepared for you. In a moment when we open the doors we will go in and begin playing." I was picturing doing a three-legged race or a burlap sack race. Wasn't that the kind of game you played on a farm? I thought I had seen that in a *Little House on the Prairie* episode. I felt a bit better. At least if it was a game, it wasn't a haunted house.

"Since we are gentlemen, we will allow you to enter first, and may I suggest when you see the game, you should start playing it right away. Got it?" I looked at Sandra and Pam. I was going to follow their lead.

"Ready, set, GO!" the guys slid the doors back to reveal two picnic tables lined with pies from end to end.

I stood at the entrance for a second thinking, "A pie

eating contest? That's a new one." In the split second as we girls paused to take in the situation, the guys ran past us, picked up pies and began throwing them at us. The proverbial light bulb went on in my brain and I knew it was war!

I dashed over to grab a whip cream laden pie and launched it at Eric. Simultaneously a pie came crashing down onto my head like a cap of sugar. There were screeches and hollers and flying frosting and projectile bits of crust filling the damp night air. It was a dessert battle between the sexes. The lines were drawn but there would be no clear winner or loser.

A minute or so after the eruption of pie violence, the calm came when no more pies were left and the fragments of pie goo on the floor were no longer salvageable as something to be smeared on the enemy. The six of us stood there wearing layers of banana cream and French silk. Sandra's sleek black hair was a white spiky Mohawk. I sported a curious whipped cream updo. No one was without 10,000 calories on his or her clothes and/or body.

"Honor?!?! Respect!?!?! Daniel McDonald! Is THIS how you show us respect?" Sandra fumed.

"I told you they might not like it," Eric squeaked nervously. Dan went into an explanation to try to pacify Sandra. I thought the pie fight was hilarious and my regard for Dan shot up tremendously.

We walked back into the house and we girls spent the next 20 minutes in the bathroom trying to clear out the cream from inside our ears and rinsed our hair out in the sink. When we were done we went back to the kitchen where Dan had dessert waiting for us—a pie.

"So where did you get the pies, Dan?" I asked.

"I made 'em."

"Are you kidding me? How many pies were there?" I was amazed to discover Dan had been baking all week in preparation for our special night. He made two dozen pies—six different varieties.

"They were all different under the cream," he proudly shared.

I eagerly ate a piece of yummy banana cream pie. Sandra in protest refused. Something must have changed because a year later, she and Dan were engaged.

They say the way to a man's heart is through his stomach. Perhaps the way to a woman's heart is through a little pie in the face.

And the raucous pie war gave me a small boost of confidence my company was sought after. I thought maybe one day soon I'd get an invite for a *real* date by one of the eligible bachelors from the pie war. But in case that never happened, I still had Rachael from high school's brother on backup duty. Despite the lack of chemistry, we pledged if we were both 35 and single, we'd just bite the bullet and marry each other.

PART III

Upward Transitions

CHAPTER 12

That Big Bay Gelding

I DIDN'T REALLY intend to get out of horse ownership when I sold Daytona, yet I did not anticipate buying another horse for a while. I enjoyed the ease and decreased expense of shareboarding. But, I have King Kong to thank for formally introducing me to a tall, dark, and handsome gentleman who became quite a prominent figure in my life.

To be exact, King Kong's suspensory ligament flared up during a February horse show, which meant I was going to have to withdraw from the competition. My genius horse trainer Joanne had an idea.

"Susan, you should ride anyway and finish out your division on DC. Dorothy's not showing today. You might as well use him. He's here in his stall."

DC had captured my attention when I went to the barn to ride King Kong. DC had recently moved in and had the most beautiful dark chocolate face with an asymmetrical blaze resembling a backward question mark. The brass nameplate on his stall read "The Don."

He would crane his long neck out of the stall and grab his nylon halter from a nearby hook with his teeth. Then he would chew on the halter like a puppy with a shoe, nodding his head up and down, shaking it. What a clown.

I had only ridden DC once during a riding lesson.

Dorothy, DC's owner, and I were jumping little courses. DC carried himself in an agitated, head upright position with Dorothy perched on his back, her reins short and tight.

Joanne called out, "I'm going to have you two switch horses for a while." I mounted DC as Joanne gave me a quick intro. "This horse has an extremely light mouth. He's only wearing a rubber snaffle—it's the mildest bit. All you have to do is squeeze like this." Joanne cupped her hands over mine on the reins and squeezed each one like a sponge.

I walked him a few strides to get used to the feel; I barely had to touch his sides with my legs and he moved forward. His trot had a prominent bounce, making posting a breeze. We trotted circles and changed directions. I had to merely look where I wanted to go and think it, barely suggesting with my rein or leg aids, and he would instantly respond. What a far cry from my first horse love, Jim Dandy! Riding DC was like getting used to a new car with more sensitive steering and brakes. His light, effortless strides felt worlds apart from King Kong's solid, purposeful ones.

Joanne told me to ride with a loopy rein and allow him to have his head. Finally, he began to lower his head and neck, and his strides became more forward and less up and down. We cantered and it was better than any amusement park ride, buoyant and springy. His head went back to pumping up and down slightly with each stride again. I felt like we were tearing around the arena, as his stride ate up the ground.

When we jumped, he was light and springy, I wondered if that's what it felt like to ride a white-tailed deer. They were common in the forest preserve adjacent to the barn, and I had seen them gracefully bound over pasture fences.

The lesson ended and Dorothy went with DC and I with Kong.

I at least had had a little bit of experience riding DC. But that was at home, in the confines of our quaint indoor arena—familiar turf. And it was under the direct tutelage of the trainer, with no one watching except the barn sparrows roosting in the arena rafters and the random cats who slinked around, patrolling for mice. This was at a show. In public! In a huge arena with spectators, an announcer and professional photographer. For me it was the Olympics!

Joanne had enough confidence for both of us, so I agreed to enter the remaining classes on "The Don." I rode well enough to place. Actually, DC performed beautifully and was a good sport. I think I was more of a passenger just trying to breathe and remember in what order to approach all eight fences of the hunter course.

As I completed my ending courtesy circle and transitioned from canter to trot and then walk, I leaned forward and patted DC's graceful brown neck. Joanne, the teen girls who worked the shows as grooms, and a few other friends from the barn came over to congratulate me. Joanne told me I needed to buy DC—we were great together and I should own him. My gut reaction was no and yes. I asked if I could lease him and found out Dorothy had to sell him so she could buy another horse. A lease was not an option.

Joanne confided in me Dorothy and DC were a terrible match. Dorothy's previous trainer had persuaded her to buy him because he was pretty and could win at shows. The trainer should have known the big gelding was too much horse for Dorothy. He was a young Thoroughbred brought up from Kentucky. Too slow to race; too hot for a timid amateur owner in her 50s.

Besides the fact I didn't have the money for a beautiful show horse. I didn't think I had the time or desire to get 100% involved again. Horses have a way of filling up all of life's crevices.

I felt guilty thinking about spending money on something extravagant and not treasuring it like I would have when I was 13, when loving a horse was the only thing that made sense in the world. I wasn't 13 anymore, and as much as I loved horses, I also wanted a relationship— with a man. Would I really be able to pursue finding a suitable someone when my life was consumed with lessons and lunging and leg wrapping?

I had noticed many older single women who came daily to the barn to ride, groom and otherwise spend time with their horse. I didn't want to be the equine version of the crazy cat lady.

"DC, the horse I rode in the show, is for sale and I want to buy him," I told my dad on the phone the day after the show. My mom picked up the phone in another room so all three of us could discuss the prospect.

Our conversation was brief and disappointment washed over me when my parents, whose advice I usually deemed as wise, said I should lease a horse instead of buying. The consensus was this was not the right time to get my next horse. "Honey, you still have horses to ride. It's cheaper and less of a commitment. Can't you just continue to lease?"

I wanted to invest my heart and the contents of my savings account. I longed to be committed. My dating life was virtually non-existent, but I could live a full life with a horse by my side. I felt they just didn't understand.

The next morning before work my dad called, which was odd since he never was the one to initiate a phone call—that was my mom's job.

"Honey, Mom and I talked it over and we think you should get the horse if you want. Here's Mom." He handed the phone off to her.

My mom explained they would like to help me financially so I could buy the horse. I was standing in the kitchen of my just-out-of-college, white-walled apartment, stunned.

I went to work and remember stopping by the desk of a middle-aged coworker whom I confided in from time to time. She was kind, and we'd chat beyond the realm of what was required for job duties. I mentioned this big news about my potential new horse, and expressed some fears about draining my meager savings account.

"Susan, I just lost one of my best friends to breast cancer. She was only 40. I think you should buy that horse and ride it and enjoy every minute you can. Life is short."

The decision was made, and pending a clean bill of health, DC was soon to be mine.

I didn't want to get my hopes up, even though Joanne assured me DC was healthy and the vet check was just a formality. I held the lead rope of this horse I was falling in love in the middle of the barn aisle as my vet took x-rays of his hooves and legs. After the exam the vet proclaimed DC as solid as a rock.

My mom gave me $3,750 to match my $3,750 from my savings account, I wrote the check for $7,500 to Dorothy and the most beautiful horse in the world became mine!

I learned sometimes love happens when you aren't looking for it or expecting it, like at a weekend horse show in which the horse you ride in on isn't the same as the one you finish on. I hoped this would be true in the romantic realm as well.

CHAPTER 13

Spring Launch

THE DAY MY niece Jamie was born, I went to the hospital to see my sister Renee's little pink papoose and share in the joy. After saying hello but not making much of an impression on the squirmy infant, I headed out to a glorious afternoon off of work. I worked from my "home office," which meant as long as I scheduled my client trainings and did follow up phone calls and visits to the stores I trained on their electronic security equipment I could pretty much pick my hours. I was 25.

A few short hours after my hospital visit, I landed in another hospital about 30 miles away.

A couple of years into owning DC, a barn scandal erupted involving a junior rider and the husband of one of the other adult women riders. The inappropriateness of the situation reverberated into a strange dynamic at the barn, and what had been a warm community of people with the same passion turned into a strange soap opera. It broke my heart. A diaspora occurred. A few other gals and I moved our horses to a new facility for a fresh start.

The goodbyes were hard, but the silver lining was the new home for our horses was exquisite.

This barn was situated a little farther out of town. To get there you had to drive up a maple-lined lane with Kentucky-style fencing on either side. There were two unique features: 1. They had an in-ground movable conveyor belt in the aisleway upon which manure was chucked and carried away to who knows where (it must have been an old dairy barn?); and 2. The indoor arena footing was shredded tires. Not sand or dirt. Black, flaky bits of old tire. It was supposedly soft and excellent for the horses—easy on their legs. The rubber substance looked like slivers of dark chocolate perfect for adorning the top of a fancy cupcake.

When I arrived at the barn, I rolled back the stall door to peek in and say hi to DC. He turned around from the flake of hay he was chewing to breathe a sweet alfalfa greeting on me. I scratched his forehead as he continued to chew and then stepped back and he resumed his hay devouring.

The arena was fairly empty—most of the traffic came during the after-school/after-work hours. I reveled in the luxury of having the stable pretty much to myself, except for one or two other horse and rider combos.

I groomed DC quickly in his stall, tacked up, and led him to the indoor arena. His demeanor was placid. Some days when he was led out of the stall, it was apparent by his elevated head carriage, and snorting nostrils he woke up on the wrong side of the stall. I blamed it on his being a Thoroughbred, a breed born to run. Much like my sister who gets crabby if she can't work out, Thoroughbreds can't think straight and act reasonably unless they get their energy out somehow. It was always a relief when he walked beside me like a well-mannered dog, heeling.

The four-beat clop of his silvery shod hooves echoed down the aisle and then disappeared completely when we crossed over into the arena. I led him to the mounting block, where he good-naturedly stood in position so I could swing aboard. Even though he was a little high strung, he stood like a gentleman every time I hopped on.

We began the first of our warm-up laps, riding at a walk on a loose rein, my hand holding the buckle. After we walked a bit, we transitioned to the posting trot, alternating being in and out of the saddle to the beat of DC's gait. Up, down. Up, down. Up, down. Butt in the air, butt in the saddle, butt in the air.

We trotted to the left, trotted to the right, trotted a circle using half of the arena, and trotted a teardrop-shaped half turn. Then I slowed DC down a bit with the slightest squeeze on the reins and began the sitting trot, which required a peculiar blend of relaxation and tightness. If I was too relaxed, I looked sloppy with my body undulating awkwardly. If I was too rigid, I'd pound on the saddle with every rise and fall of the trotting motion—not a good feeling for DC nor me. I practiced my relaxation and breathing. It was a good ride.

DC and I took a break to walk some more and gear up for cantering. DC's canter was highly comedic. Not necessarily to watch, although he did look like an enlarged merry-go-round horse with a lot of up and down movement in addition to a very forward stride. This was not a canter for a new rider or someone with motion sickness. There was a trick to sitting it quietly and retaining a look of elegance. He was animated and exuberant. His canter frequently unleashed my giggles. His canter was the essence of joy.

We picked up the left lead canter ONE, two, three; ONE, two, three; ONE, two, three. Very light and rhythmical. DC was relaxed and so was I. His canter that day was reminiscent of a Quarter Horse lope—long-necked, low-headed and lazy. It definitely was a bit out of character from the carousel horse canter which was the norm. We transitioned to the trot and changed direction, ready to canter to the right. I rode with an almost western-length rein. It was not a great idea.

I nudged DC's left side with my left heel and simultaneously sat tall and squeezed a little on the right rein. He launched into a mellow, yet comfortable right lead canter. His head carriage was still low, quite a dramatic transformation from the extremely high and tense head and neck he had when I first rode him in the riding lesson years earlier.

A few strides into our initial canter departure as we were rounding a curve on a short side of the arena, DC tripped and fell down onto his knees. I catapulted over his neck like a ragdoll, landing face first on the shredded tire footing. My black velvet riding helmet was still on my head, but the impact forced the brim down onto the bridge of my nose.

I turned over on the ground, shoved my helmet up so I

could see, and lay face up. DC was standing right next to me, muzzle hovering a few inches above me as if to inspect my condition and apologize. I was relieved he was standing. I was also relieved he did not somersault onto me, which was a huge concern during the millisecond I was airborne.

As I began to process what had just happened seconds before, I realized I felt incredibly congested. I knew my face was dirty; I brushed off the arena bits from my cheeks and forehead while lying down. A middle-aged woman ran over to me and kneeled next to me to ask if I was okay. I said yes, only because I could tell I was alive and I hadn't passed out. She said I should stay put for a few minutes. Someone else came to get DC and took him back to his stall. He had a couple of minor cuts on his knees, but was just fine. That was a blessing.

The barn owner was summoned, and she kneeled down and chatted with me for a while as I was still resting on the ground. She asked me who I was, what day it was, and how many fingers she was holding up.

When she deemed me ready to get up, I rose and immediately walked into the restroom to wash my filthy face. I was unprepared to see in the mirror my nose askew to the left! The small bump below the bridge of my nose, a family trait from my mother's side, was gone. I had never really liked my nose very much, especially as a teenager when appearance and self-esteem were one and the same.

I'd traded in the bump for a left leaning nose. It *had* to be broken. And there was a small gash right above my nose from my helmet slipping forward.

While my mom (who'd come to pick me up) and I waited in the ER, I was confident I would have to have a nose job to correct my nasal condition. I couldn't go through life with permanent congestion and a slightly sideways schnoz. Instead of experiencing devastation, I was supremely overjoyed. This was the best thing to happen to me in quite a while!

I began searching for my perfect new nose as I scoured through the waiting room magazines. It was tricky finding a good profile view of a model's nose from one of the ads. I couldn't show the doctor a front view nose and expect him to interpret what the side angle looked like.

My name was called and I gleefully went to radiology. The x-rays proved I had indeed broken my nose and would therefore be entitled to plastic surgery paid for by my insurance, thanks to DC!

I learned a few things in the two weeks between my fall and the time of my rhinoplasty.

1. MAC has the best makeup for covering purple eyes.
2. More people have had nose jobs than I realized.

Having a broken nose wasn't bad. I could still drive, write, eat, and do pretty much everything except ride (the only bummer). I even got time off of work. I can't blame my company for not wanting to send me out to visit customers. I looked like a cosmetology school test subject gone wrong. The entire area from eyelashes to eyebrows on both sides of my face took on a bright purple hue. It appeared as though I had gone overboard with eggplant eyeshadow. I'd been known to wear eye shadow to excess in my teen years, but I would not have caked on the purple. It's not a good color for a strawberry blonde. And there was a red cut on the bridge of my nose.

I went to a plastic surgeon for a consultation and learned I had to wait two weeks for surgery. The doctor could not do the procedure to correct my deviated septum and literally set me straight until all the swelling had gone down. I knew I couldn't take a two week vacation from work, so I visited the MAC counter at a nearby mall. A gay friend from high school who knew everything cool about fashion and cosmetics had mentioned one time MAC got started as makeup for runway models. I thought maybe they'd have some heavy-duty concealer to make my weird face somewhat normal.

I walked into Woodfield Mall a purple-eyed freak, and I emerged from the shopping trip my normal-looking self thanks to the dear sales girl who waited on me. She'd actually studied makeup in Los Angeles, and learned how to make actors become outlandish characters with the right cosmetics and prostheses. It stood to reason she could transform a face-plant victim with blazing violet eyelids into a regular person. And she did, with a little help from a magical foundation in a compact that had to be blasted with a hair dryer in order for it to emit small dewy beads of flesh-colored cream. Once cream-ified, she used a small sponge to dab the miracle makeup onto my purple parts and make them look natural again. It was amazing.

My surgery drew near, and while I did not relish the thought of being anesthetized, I did want to welcome my new nose to the world and begin riding again. I finally found my perfect nose, and it belonged to supermodel Christy Turlington. After paging through a dozen or so magazines, I found a Calvin Klein ad which portrayed Christy from the side. Her nose was regal and aristocratic, not too cutesy turned up or too small.

I showed my doctor the pictures of my desired nose and he assured me he would do his best, but each person's face calls for a different kind of nose. What looked good on Christy might not be appropriate on me, but he would use her classic-looking olfactory organ as the standard by which to fashion mine. And so he did.

I wouldn't find out for sure until the day I got to re-move the cast. Yes, the nose cast. After my operation I stayed at my parents' house so they could keep an eye on me, feed me and administer meds. The days of recovery were a haze except for the memory of sleeping upright in my mom's recliner in the den and watching Black Beauty on VHS. I wept and wept at the tragedies befalling such a good horse—I felt his losses on a personal level. I think it was the meds talking.

On June 13, my friend Gail (my co-conspirator with Penny at the horse show all those years before) who had become a nurse offered to join me for the nose reveal— the day the cast would come off. It was her birthday.

On the way to the doctor's office, Gail listened as I rattled on about how I dreamed the cast was removed and I had Jimmy Durante's nose. I didn't even really know who Jimmy Durante was, but I had heard my parents mention him and I knew he was famous for having an enormous nose. In my dream I said, "Doctor, put the cast back on! I would rather wear a cast forever than live life with Jimmy Durante's nose!"

I also told her the agony of having the gauze removed from my nostrils, sinuses and brain a few days after the procedure. I was relieved to get the stuffing removed from my nose so I wasn't relegated to Darth Vader mouth breathing. No one had adequately prepared me for this pain or the mammoth-sized boogers soon to follow.

On my first post-op follow up, the surgeon removed the gauze that was packed into my nasal cavities since the surgery a few days prior. The doctor tugged at the gauze peeking out from one nostril and pulled. It felt like barbed wire being extracted from my face. And it kept coming! About a yard of it. It was like a magician pulling an endless ribbon of tied scarves out of his sleeve. The removed gauze was not so gauzy as it was coated in dried blood.

Gail listened as I described how nervous I was about not actually having Christy Turlington's nose, but the nose of a little piggy. Every day I wore the cast I would stand before the large mirror on the family room wall. I would get as close to it as I could to study my appearance; I was trying to gauge the "after" version of my face. I was disheartened when I noticed my nostrils were flared out and the tip of my nose was turned up. Turned up to the point of showing the world the two cavernous nostrils I now possessed. I didn't know what was worse, looking like Miss Piggy or Jimmy Durante. At least Miss Piggy was undeniably feminine.

The great part about having a best friend like Gail is not just she would still like me regardless of my nose, but she would go to the appointment with me, listen to my drama and radiate her calming influence. It was even better knowing a trained medical professional was entering the room with me.

The moment of truth came when the surgeon removed my nose cast. It turned out my nose looked beautiful—better than I could have imagined. I loved it. And I looked normal, except for the mild dark circles under my eyes, but they were no match for my new MAC foundation.

My nose eventually healed and my family and friends became accustomed to it; I began to ride a few weeks after the cast was removed. I got my confidence back, but a freak accident does stay in one's mind. The tapes still played when I asked for a right lead canter on DC. I have since made a point to ride with more contact on the reins when cantering. I don't know if that would have made any difference in my situation. The past is past and I can't change the way I rode, but in the end it turned out okay. I got the nose of a supermodel. And in time, my new look would yield a new attitude and pave the way for unexpected attention from the gentlemen.

CHAPTER 14

Irish Horse Holiday

IN THE HEART of every Midwesterner there's an urge to leave the brutal winter with its six months of gray and journey the way of the gold prospectors. The gold we desire is sunshine, and I was going to head west to find it. A few months after my new nose took residency on my face, I moved away from suburban Chicago to Southern California.

My company had an opening for my exact job in L.A. Instead of training a territory consisting of suburban Chicago and all of Illinois, Wisconsin, Iowa, Indiana, and Minnesota, I would be traveling from Los Angeles to Santa Barbara—a more condensed region. This meant no more business trips flying on school bus-sized planes and no more hotel stays in various bland suburbs. I would no longer be dining at ubiquitous chains like the Olive Garden alone.

Instead I would hobnob with clients in Beverly Hills, Burbank, and Santa Monica, with overnight trips along California's Central Coast! Not a bad trade. My familiar job took on a new, potentially glamorous spin.

DC moved to a boarding stable 20 minutes away from my new apartment in the San Gabriel Valley. His journey from Chicago to Lexington, Lexington to Dallas, and then Dallas straight to Los Angeles via a shipping company specializing in hauling race horses took a toll. When I first saw him at the new barn, he had lost weight and was very nervous. I felt guilty dragging him to California, putting him through such stress; I didn't know any better at the time.

Happily, DC quickly gained weight on his new diet of alfalfa cubes. I didn't understand why there wasn't fresh hay and why the horses weren't fed grain, but he adapted well. In fact, I think he put on a bit of extra weight to the point of looking like a Thelwell pony from the British kids' book series.

Through my small network of fellow Midwesterner 20-somethings, I made a new friend who also loved to ride. Holly, a native Californian, worked as a personal assistant to the famous romance writer Sidney Sheldon. She regularly rode horses on the trails in Griffith Park. We enthusiastically talked horse whenever we saw each other, which was every Sunday at church.

Some people dream of beaches in Hawaii or the Caribbean, but not me. I fantasize about expansive fields. I had always dreamed of riding in Ireland; I wanted to gallop across the vast farmland of the Emerald Isle. I shared this longing with Holly and she said she was game for such a journey. I had a travel partner to make this happen!

Holly researched the trip and discovered an agency specializing in horseback riding vacations around the world. There were various Ireland vacations from which to choose. There were old castles to stay in and take daily lessons in an arena and then ride on trails. Some stays specialized in cross country jumping. Holly rode western so it probably wouldn't have been a wise idea.

The trip that wooed Holly was the Sligo Trail Ride. This was a self-guided tour across County Sligo from one bed and breakfast to another; each night we'd be staying at a different location. Being an independent gal and not wanting to be micromanaged while we rode, Holly wanted the freedom and flexibility of the on-your-own trail ride. Maybe we'd meet some hot Irishmen who had been riding since they were wee lads!

In June of 1998 we flew from Los Angeles to London. Our bags did not arrive with us, but that didn't stop us from seeing Le Miserables in the theatre district. We also dropped by the third floor Notting Hill penthouse of of Sidney Sheldon's London home. He requested Holly deliver something to him from his L.A. base.

I knew a few things about Mr. Sheldon. He was extremely wealthy as the best-selling author of novels I had never read, and about 80 at the time, but still working. He had won an Oscar, Emmy, and Tony. And I was a minor character in his most recent book—at least my last name was used, thanks to Holly.

As Sidney wrote his novels, he would think of the main characters but leave the names of the minor characters up to his assistant. There was a Miriam in the story who needed a last name, so Holly named her Friedland. Sadly, my character ended up dying of a drug overdose. Another friend of ours from church was named in the book—he got to be a U.S. Senator.

There was one point during our visit when Holly and Sidney's wife left the room momentarily. I was alone on the couch visiting with Mr. Sheldon. It was a little awkward. I wished I had read one of his books so I'd have something intelligent to say, but romance novels weren't my thing.

I was happy to find out he and I had one thing in common—he was from Illinois too. Born in Chicago before the Depression, he attended Northwestern University where my grandmother had gone. He asked me what kind of work I did, and I told him I was in a customer training role for a company that sold electronic surveillance equipment. He asked if I worked with computers. I said yes and he assumed I ttrained people how to use computers, which wasn't really the case. He said he had no idea how to use a computer, not even turn one on. And that is why Holly was such a valuable asset to him.

I felt much more comfortable by the end of our visit. I realized even though the Sheldons were wealthy beyond belief and Sidney was from the glamorous world of old Hollywood (he was friends with Cary Grant), they were just people and a sweet elderly couple. Maybe someday I would find someone with whom I could grow old and reminisce about the 1980s. And just maybe that man was in England or Ireland!

Our tardy bags arrived in London in time for them to

accompany us on our flights to Dublin and then Sligo. I was disappointed no one asked to look at my passport as we entered Ireland. The people in the Sligo airport were cheery and talkative. Even our chirpy taxi driver. He was happy to learn we were from Los Angeles and quick to tell us he honeymooned there—in Culver City, which I thought odd since it's not even coastal.

The upbeat cabby dropped us off at the farm, and the setting was *exactly* like the images of all the how-to horse books I read in the '80s, published in the UK.

Our host oddly enough, was not Irish but German. He had none of the hospitality of Sidney Sheldon or the taxi driver. He was tall, unsmiling and intimidating. He drove us down the road to a bed and breakfast where we stashed our bags and changed into riding clothes. He then took us back down the road to meet the horses.

The horse selected for me, Gweebarra, was a mid-sized chestnut gelding with a white blaze and the thickest tail I had ever seen. He stood politely while I approached him in the field and put on his apple-red nylon halter. The guide instructed us to put our steeds in vacant box stalls and gave them each a bucketful of grain. (I thought you weren't supposed to eat before exercising, but I didn't dare ask questions.)

We groomed the horses and tacked up. The saddle pads were rubber which I'd never seen before or since. The girths were made of string. I had seen those in my old black and white riding books. I had entered a horsekeeping time warp.

A German teen (maybe the stern man's daughter?) led

our ride, which was more of a test drive to ensure we were partnered up with the right mount. Two girls also in their late 20s from London joined us; they were on holiday too. We left the farm, clopping down the paved road and then turned onto a grassy lane eventually leading us to the beach.

The only thing beachy about the spot was the Atlantic water next to it. This was a rocky shore, impassable by my standards. Gray stones ranged in size from grapefruit to loaves of banana bread. I thought of DC at home and how he would not be able to walk even a yard on this ground. No problem for Gweebarra. The kindly copper horse lowered his head and picked his way carefully through the rocks. He may not have been as tall or handsome as DC, but he was amazing.

After we cleared the jutted obstacle course and reached sand that would pass as a beach by California standards, our leader questioned, "Would you like to go for a gallop?"

I couldn't hear the British girls, but Holly and I said something in the affirmative—we'd like to trot and *then* canter. We weren't anticipating a gallop from a standstill, but our guide turned jockey and took off ahead of us. Gweebarra and Killen, Holly's bay, morphed into racing Thoroughbreds. We really had no choice in the matter.

The first few strides of the gallop were frightening. I had done a lot more worrying as a rider since the accident where I broke my nose. Nervousness transformed into elation, however, when I trusted and let the chestnut go. I loosened my death grip on the reins and let them follow my horse's head movement with a subtle back and forth give and take. I crouched down, hovering above Gweebarra's neck. His auburn mane flapped, a banner in the wind.

We thundered so fast the green hills on one side and thin strip of taupe sand on the other side blurred in my peripheral vision. Tears flowed down my face from the sheer speed. Perhaps a few were in memory of the carefree days I spent as a young girl riding Jim Dandy in the acres of wondrous forest preserve. Joy, freedom, and independence were palpable then and in this moment. The vacation had already exceeded my expectations.

After our gallop we traversed through hilly dunes and a pasture populated by cows and sheep. This was Ireland exactly how I pictured it. Over the next several days, Holly and I adventured with our mounts near the sea and over the moor. With the exception of meeting a 60s-ish widower named Mickey Joe at a local pub, we did not encounter any men on our rural Irish vacation. And in the end, it was okay.

PART IV

On the Circuit

CHAPTER 15

Paris Before 30

"OH, EMILY!" THE redheaded actress squealed from the stage of the university auditorium, "I can hardly believe we're going!"

"I know, Cornelia! Just think, we're actually going on a ship across the wide Atlantic to *Paris*!!! Our parents' ship may be more luxurious, but here we are alone—emancipated! Our diaries for the summer of 1910 will be perfectly *scandalous*!" Emily sighed wistfully as she gazed into the audience.

I was Emily. My high school best friend, Shelly, was Cornelia.

The year after the Valentine's banquet that wasn't, Shelly and I represented our high school in a speech competition in the duet acting category. We portrayed Emily and Cornelia from the story *Our Hearts Were Young and Gay*, a memoir set in the early 1900s. This tale tells of two recently graduated high school girls who voyage to Europe via ocean liner and are on a quest to be cosmopolitan. While on board, however, instead of exuding sophistication, they find themselves in awkward situations such as inadvertently stealing shoes and knocking a fellow passenger overboard. We were a live stage version of Lucy and Ethel.

Shelly and I won both the state competition and the national competition, and as a result, vowed we would go to Paris together before we were 30, just like our characters Emily and Cornelia.

Shelly went off to college in Ohio and then to teach English in China for three years. I stayed in Illinois and stuck around the Chicago suburbs post-graduation trying to figure out a meaningful line of work. We slowly lost touch until Christmas 1999.

The details are hazy, but somehow we reconnected and met at an Italian restaurant to catch up and reminisce. Shelly was in grad school and on the brink of engagement to a German computer guy named Stephan whom she met at church. I was going to grad school full time and in my first year of teaching in Southern California. We hadn't seen each other in several years, but we laughed and shared stories as if no time had passed.

Shelly tentatively brought up our teenage plan to travel to France to see if I was still game, and revealed her boyfriend's best friend who looked like Sting and was a violin maker lived in Paris, and we could probably stay at his apartment.

I'll admit other than our high school promise to see Paris, I hadn't given it much thought as a vacation destination. It seemed *everyone* loved Paris. I thought it must surely be overrated. I have some level of conversational Spanish and would have preferred to go someplace like Argentina or maybe even Rome. But this new wrinkle—the handsome violin maker with the accent as a possible host turned me almost instantly into a Francophile. Besides, I had always wanted to see the Eiffel Tower.

Summer came and Shelly and I set off for our dream trip. We met at O'Hare Airport and instantly reverted to high school giggles and tried to appear chic, as though we traveled to Paris all the time.

We devoured the Paris guidebook during the nine hour flight, deciding on which tourist destinations we absolutely *had* to see. It was a bit disconcerting, however, when the in-flight entertainment featured a soft news segment about jerky. The reporter gave a history of jerky and interviewed jerky lovers, trying to uncover the popularity of this all-American treat. There was a little old man from Appalachia who was interviewed and listed off types of jerky he made. Shelly and I were horrified when he named raccoon and skunk jerky. We felt Americans were totally misrepresented and worried the French passengers would lump us into the same category as the jerky man. So not *tres chic*!

Shelly kept reiterating how incredibly good-looking Kolton was, and he drove all the girls wild. That information coupled with restlessness from sitting in a small space for what seemed like an eternity did a number on me. I couldn't get off the plane fast enough.

We collected our luggage, had our passports stamped, and met the mysterious Kolton near the exit doors of

Charles de Gaulle.

Kolton wasn't at all what I pictured—Sting is blond, Kolton had darker hair—but he was tall and soft spoken. He led us to the Metro and we rode off to his two bedroom apartment, not too far from Notre Dame.

Shelly and I settled into the spare room and freshened. The jet lag had not hit me since I was thrilled to be in the City of Lights in the company of my best friend and our intriguing host. Kolton suggested we make dinner and have a picnic by the river. He insisted we should see Notre Dame at night. My two companions threw together a simple pasta meal in his miniature hallway kitchen. They packed the dinner and we headed out to a brasserie to pick up a bottle of wine.

The Parisian neighborhood was just how I had pictured it! I could easily envision myself living there, wearing a black linen dress and Jackie O sunglasses, walking a terrier while carrying both a bouquet of flowers and a baguette on one arm. I knew nothing about wine, so Shelly and Kolton selected a red to complement our pasta.

The three of us small talked and walked along the Seine River on the wide concrete lane for pedestrians and bicyclists. At one spot there were steps leading down to the river's edge. Below us several couples were swing dancing! There was a boombox blasting big band music and my heart leapt. We sat down on the inclined embankment, which gave us a perfect view of the water and the dancers below. And there we picnicked. As each swing song ended and the dancers rearranged to new partners, I was antsy and remorseful. If only I had taken French instead of Spanish in college! If only I had the nerve to walk up to one of the men and ask them to dance.

"That looks like fun! Kolton, do you dance?" I was hopeful. Kolton said he didn't know how, which was a tragedy for me. I was in Paris, on the river, it was a beautiful night, and the locals were doing *my* dance! I had taken East Coast Swing lessons a couple of years earlier, during the revival of Big Band music thanks to The Gap's catchy Jump Jive and Wail commercial, and had gotten hooked.

The moon began to rise and the sky transformed from smoky blue to navy. Had I known there was swing scene in Paris, I could have brought my dancing shoes and maybe even a French phrasebook so I could learn how to ask a man to dance.

While my internal debate waged regarding whether or not I should just walk up to a dancer and smile and extend my hand, regardless of the language barrier, I noticed Kolton kneeling on a stair step talking to one of the dancers. I didn't think anything of it. I thought maybe he ran into a friend. A few minutes later Kolton and the "friend" came back over to us.

"*Excusez* moi! Would you like to dahnce?"

I thanked the man who became my dance partner for the next song, grinned and extended my hand. The Parisian led me to the "floor." We held hands, assuming open position and smiled at each other.

"My name is Felipe. I am sorry. I am not a good dancer," my partner said in an accent, as sweet as a chocolate croissant.

Felipe was being modest. He was good. If one of my

hands were free while we danced, I think I just might have pinched myself. "I'm in Paris, a houseguest of a handsome violin maker, I just had a picnic on the Seine and now I'm dancing under a full moon with a Frenchman with a buttery accent. I LOVE Paris!"

When the dance was over, another dark-haired Frenchman approached me for the next song. I told him to wait and took off my sensible walking shoes—shoes clearly not meant to swivel and spin. I danced barefoot with him and then with a couple more partners. After a few more songs I went back to my picnic spot next to Shelly and Kolton, winded, with dirty, scuffed feet, yet feeling so alive. I could get used to Paris. Did they have any riding stables nearby? Would DC travel by plane well?

A COUPLE OF days into my trip, I realized I was turning into one of *those* girls—the ones who fell for the dreamy violin maker. It started at the breakfast table over toast and coffee. Shelly was in the bathroom getting dolled up and I was alone with Kolton. Black and white photographs he'd taken hung on the wall like a gallery. A guitar rested on a stand. I liked the vibe of his apartment and personality.

Besides both knowing Shelly and both having lived in suburban Chicago, Kolton and I had one other commonality. I'm German too (going way, way back). I hesitated to say I'm German because I had no affinity for or connection to the culture. I can't speak the language, I had never been to the country, and I wasn't really fond of the cuisine with all the sausages and meats.

I explained to Kolton my dad had been looking into family history recently, and was excited to find out I'd be staying with Kolton because he's German. He wanted me to ask if Kolton had ever heard of a place called Mecklenberg, the place my great-grandfather was from. I never knew him.

Kolton's gray-green eyes grew wide. He knew exactly where Mecklenburg was. It was very close to where he grew up—a small town. And he'd never heard of any Americans who hailed from that area. Kolton retrieved a small box filled with pictures and pulled out a black and white photograph of a pastoral landscape. It could have been the fields my grandparents farmed in Harmony, Illinois. There were acres and acres of flat land with a dark line of trees edging the field.

It all made sense. The picture told me why, a few generations back, the German immigrants settled in Illinois and other parts of the Midwest. It looked like home.

Kolton opened up and told me about the land, about when East was divided from West, about his uncle who narrowly escaped being forced to join the SS forces. He spoke in relaxed, low tones with the very slightest English accent. I could listen to him all day.

Shelly, looking bright and fresh and ready to explore pulled up an empty chair and began to eat her breakfast. "So, today we're going to Versailles, right, Kolton?"

He nodded and said yes. I felt sheepish. I wondered if Shelly could tell from the look on my face I was swooning. I knew she was trying to set Kolton up with another one of her friends. When I mentioned to her later I was developing a little crush on our host she dismissed it.

Versailles was as glorious as the books depict, but even more so when there with a handsome bachelor. Kolton rented a rowboat to take us around on the man-made rectangular pond. He rowed us as we relaxed and drank in the luxurious view of flowers and greenery. It was like a scene out of a Jane Austen novel.

The rest of the day was perfect. And so was the next. We went to the Pantheon and the crypt where Victor Hugo's bones are interned. We saw Foucault's pendulum. When we visited Luxembourg Gardens, we got caught in a heavy rainstorm without an umbrella. The three of us ran shrieking—actually only two of us were shrieking, Kolton was too masculine and understated—to the closest Metro underground stop.

As we ran down the stairs breathless and sopping wet, Kolton suggested we head to a café to have a snack and get out of the rain. I loved how he thought.

The last night, the three of us got dressed up and went to a swanky restaurant, La Coupule. I dreaded leaving my new favorite city and my new favorite person. Shelly and I sat there in our dressy clothes feeling very much like children since we couldn't read anything on the menu. Kolton was our dad, interpreting the dinner selections and telling us which ones we might like and which ones to avoid. I think we exasperated our waiter by the scores of questions, but he had a sense of humor about it. As did Kolton. Everything I had heard about bad service in Paris was wrong.

That night I could hardly sleep. I had contracted what so many other girls before me had when in the presence of the German violin maker. I had a full-blown junior high crush, charged with the energy of ripe estrogen. How could I say goodbye to such a kind, funny, intelligent, handsome man? I wondered if when I left it would be like nothing had ever happened. I would be just a random houseguest—a friend of a friend.

The morning we left, Shelly and I hugged and thanked Kolton for his hospitality. He had to go to work, and so it was a quick goodbye. The good news was Kolton promised to attend Stephan and Shelly's wedding, which was going to be in December in Chicago. I would be there too. I wasn't sure if Kolton was the kind of man who kept his word and I'd see him in six short months, but I was comforted by the fact Shelly entrusted him to transport her recent purchase—an oversized Le Creuset pot—back to the States when he came for the wedding. My hope was I had made an impression and my absence would make his heart grow fonder.

CHAPTER 16

Showing it Alone

AFTER MOVING TO California, my time for riding faded when I quit my corporate training job to become a teacher. I was tired of traveling. I was already teaching people as a trainer, but why not teach people I could actually see more than once and not have to drive three hours, stay in some Hampton Inn and dine alone at Chili's?

I enrolled in a teacher education program at a local graduate school, and in the span of 14 months I had earned a master's degree in education, written a thesis, put in 25 observation hours, taken a few subject matter competency tests, student taught, went to a job fair and landed a teaching job. So I was actually a first year teacher and a grad student simultaneously. I thought if I hated teaching, at least I would have earned an MA, a welcome addition to any resume.

About my third year teaching, things settled down and I was riding DC enough again so I contemplated taking him to a little local show. Someone at my barn had a trailer and she was going to take her horse, so she offered me a ride. I had never done a horse show alone before. By that I mean without my mom, sister, and especially trainer. I was a seasoned horsewoman and though my show career had been on hiatus, I certainly knew how to walk, trot, and canter a horse. I viewed this as a chance to challenge myself and have a "learning experience."

The day before the show, I bathed DC and said a prayer he wouldn't lie down in a pile of his own brownish green apples and not sleep so soundly that tiny cream-colored shavings would cling to his fuzz of a forelock and mane and tail. I rubbed his forehead and scratched his chin a bit and gave him a kiss goodnight, and took home his saddle pad to wash.

The next morning I arrived at the barn early. The row of horses I had to pass all had their heads down, intent on eating their breakfast.

When I called his name, DC courteously took a few steps toward me, ears perked, still chewing, and then returned to the more interesting pile of green stems on the ground. I let him continue to eat as I squatted down to wrap his legs with puffy white pads and black standing wraps. I had already made sure to take only my essential brushes, a hoof pick and fly spray in my yellow plastic brush box. I put the saddle, girth, bridle, and brush box in my car. I was good to go. Except I had forgotten my saddle pad. Which I realized once I got DC settled at the showgrounds.

One of DC's shortcomings was he could not be tied. If he was tied, he would pull back and break his halter.

Better to have a broken halter than a broken horse, though. He sported a nylon halter with a leather crown piece so the halter would snap in an emergency.

Because this was essentially a step above a schooling show, I didn't have to braid him. I had rented a stall since I could not tie him to the trailer. I was the only one who'd rented a stall. Everyone else had someone to take turns holding their horse. I walked past several horses tied to trailers, happily munching from a haynet. I didn't say it to them but thought, *Don't you know all it would take is one quick tug and you could be free?*

I threw some hay into the box stall, which was a few hundred feet away from the arena. DC whinnied and whinnied and whinnied a series of shrill calls. He was so loud and obvious. It was embarrassing.

I found someone who loaned me a saddle pad and then decided I should turn DC loose in the round pen, also about 300 feet from the show ring. Maybe he could get rid of some of his nervous energy by frolicking for a few minutes. He did just that, huffing and puffing and shaking his head. To my horror, the horse show announcer announced, "The round pen is not open during the show. You need to remove your horse from the round pen." Now I was not only the lady with the horse who wouldn't shut up, but I was the rule breaker. Which was odd since I'm very much a rule follower in real life. It's just unwritten rules I'm no good at. Had there been a sign, "No turnout," everything would have been good.

Somewhere in the midst of this chaos, Gabriel showed up. Not the angel, but a friend from church. Gabriel was a single dad I had gotten to know through our young adults ministry. He had always wanted to learn how to ride horses and so he asked me to join him a few weeks earlier when he embarked on a mission to purchase boots and a riding helmet so he could take riding lessons from his sister-in-law who ran a small stable. I had never seen Gabriel ride, but knew he was a beginner.

I needed to head over to the show secretary's table to register for my classes and get my number, so I left DC in his charge. Although he was green around horses, I figured he was a guy and therefore strong. I assumed in his limited riding experience, he probably knew how to hold a horse. It couldn't be that tricky to hold a lead rope. But I hadn't accounted for just how tricky it can be to hold the lead of an unsettled horse at a show.

When I started filling in the papers, DC started his fretful whinnying again. One of the ladies at the registration table made a snide remark about "that bay horse." As I filled in the registration form I said, "I'm trying to enter 'that bay horse' of mine into the hunter class," hoping to make her feel embarrassed. But it was my turn again as someone shouted, "Loose horse!"

I turned and surmised DC had spooked and pulled away from Gabriel as he was trotting proudly, much like the Black Stallion in the scene where the boy was trying to tame him. DC sure was beautiful when he was loose. Thankfully, DC's wild freedom was short lived as a nearby Good Samaritan successfully grabbed the dangling leadrope.

I thanked the helpful stranger and told Gabriel not to

worry about it. I was the one who at this point was a bundle of nerves: my horse had been broadcasting his unease by whinnying across the whole showgrounds, I had been publicly busted over the loudspeaker for lunging him in the round pen, and now he had been *the* "loose horse!" What was going to happen when I mounted and actually rode him in the show ring? Maybe it was stupid to think I could go to a horse show by myself. Where was Joanne when I needed her? And my mom?

To make matters worse, I had noticed earlier there was a spectator camped out at the far end of the show ring with a large blue beach umbrella. In most every arena I had ridden in, DC would select one specific spot of the arena as his personal nemesis. If he were feeling very spunky he would let out a full-blown spook, snorting and shying away from the terrifying corner. If he were feeling a little more subdued he might simply drift in toward the middle of the arena or stay near the rail, but turn his face slightly opposite of the proper bend, suspiciously eyeing the scary region of the rail. I would prepare for such shenanigans by maintaining solid yet gentle contact on the outside rein and keeping my inside leg very close to the girth, putting pressure on his side, in an attempt to keep him straight. And I would try to focus my attention on a point beyond the scary spot. And breathe. The irony in riding is there is so much going on behind the scenes: thoughts, subtle muscle movements, ring strategy in an attempt to make for a beautiful ride, portraying the horse as though he is moving effortlessly and everything is his own idea.

Gabriel had another event to go to and so he said goodbye just as I was about to start riding.

When I mounted DC against my better judgment, it was as though I had come to rest on a wad of nerves, not my lovely equine companion of 10 years. My heart was fluttering even though my brain was telling me to be calm and communicate confidence to my horse. He needed me to be the adult in this situation.

DC held his head high, like a sentinel scanning the king's domain. I walked him in the most forward walk he was capable of to the schooling area and began warming up for impending disaster. Earlier in our show career, I lunged DC for about 40 minutes at the trot to get him to relax. And by the end of the session he was mellow enough to behave civilly. I did not have that luxury this time. Instead, I attempted to recreate what had been a successful strategy Joanne had taught me a decade earlier. And so began our marathon trotting exercise. The tricky part was I knew if I trotted him too much, I would be useless, as my fitness level was no match for his.

Right as I was about to depart the schooling area to sheepishly ride "that bay horse" into the show ring for our first class, a familiar, cheery, "Hi Susan!" broke into my internal pep talk.

I could have cried. Dana and Patrick, two dear friends who didn't even know each other, had showed up at the same time to support me. Dana had her camera in hand.

"I'm about ready to go in. This should be interesting." I pointed out where they could stand along the rail to have a prime view of the forthcoming entertainment.

My horse, who had been a bundle of raw energy, decided to use his power for good once inside the show ring. The announcer intoned, "You are now being judged at a walk."

I took a deep breath and tried to shove my heels down further and stretch my spine up taller. I put on a smile. Not a senior picture or wedding day smile, but the corners of my mouth turned up a bit, reflecting the sheer delight and pleasure it was to be on such a grand steed.

There were only about five other riders in the arena, and I did my best to space myself out so DC and I could dazzle the judge. We neared the umbrella lady on our first lap and DC didn't bat an eyelash. In fact, he perked his ears forward and kept looking straight ahead, very receptive to my subtle squeezes on the reins.

When the judge wasn't looking, I talked to DC. I don't think he needed any reassurances, but I did. I knew if I talked, I would have to breathe. And if I had to breathe, my body would hopefully relax.

We began to trot at the announcer's bidding. I could feel the correct diagonal, but still glanced down with my eyes only, keeping my head level and looking ahead. I was fine, but didn't want to take anything for granted. DC's springiness popped me out of the saddle ever so slightly and I went forward with the motion gently for a millisecond until I sat down to repeat the cycle of posting: UP, down, UP, down.

The judge called for a walk and I knew what was next. So did DC, but he didn't let on. After a few strides where I regrouped, shoving my heels down against the stirrup irons, shortening my reins an inch and caught a glimpse of my two dedicated fans standing at the edge of the arena. "Riders, please canter your horses. Canter." I barely grazed DC's right side with the heel of my boot, giving a little squeeze to the left rein, a squeeze just like the end of prayer when you're holding someone's hand in church. My show horse pushed off his hind end and burst forward into a left lead canter. "Good boy!" I whispered. He flickered his ears back for a second, listening to me, and then focused his ears forward again to show off for the judge. I sat tall and proud. None of the earlier snafus mattered—the forgotten saddle pad, the announcer scolding me about using the round pen, DC's blaring whinnies across the showgrounds. We were there to perform for the judge and for the crowd. But mostly for each other.

DC's elegant stride swallowed the ground and I maneuvered around other slower horse and rider combinations. It wasn't a race, but there was something gratifying about forging ahead of the others. My carousel horse kept the same rhythmical hoofbeats going until the judge called for a walk. I saw down deeper in the saddle and pressed all of my fingers firmly together on the reins to make them signal the transition. DC slowed down and resumed a forward, showy walk.

The judge called for a reverse and I worried approaching the umbrella from the new side might be cause for reaction. Not so. We repeated the same energetic trot followed by the right lead canter. I preferred cantering to the left since my nose break accident had occurred at the right lead canter. Alas, the entire ride should have been videoed because it was textbook perfect. I still had low expectations. After all, I had been the show black sheep.

DC stood like a gentleman as we awaited the results. He turned a bit to the left and a bit to the right to check out his competition close up. He chewed the silver snaffle bit just a little and then looked at the judge with his ears pointed forward. I swear he was posing for her.

There were six of us in the class so I figured we'd at least get a ribbon. The judge revealed the placings beginning with 6th place. Our number was not called. He went through all the other placings then called, "In first place, number 282, Susan Friedland riding Adonis."

I leaned forward to accept our blue ribbon. DC and I trotted to the gate where my friends were waiting.

"Congratulations, Susan!" Dana cheered in her mild Louisiana sing song. Patrick smiled, congratulated me, chuckled and congratulated DC. DC was less interested in the words of praise and pats than in sniffing the new people to see if they had any carrots. I gave Dana the ribbon and returned to the arena for the next class: equitation.

My confidence had risen 16 hands high!

The second class was almost the same as the first, although I was more relaxed. And when it was over we had won another blue. By the end of the day I had won the championship for my division. Even though it was "just" a schooling show, I was as delighted as if I had won at Madison Square Garden. DC was quirky and sometimes unruly, but I had him mostly figured out. We were a true team. My heart was bursting with love and my spirit with joy. It didn't matter if I was still single. I knew with whom and where I belonged.

The best part of this horse show was two weeks later, a friend from my barn said, "Susan, I got an email from the organizer of the schooling show. They put out a monthly newsletter and she was wondering if she could get a picture of you and DC to include in the next issue."

I smugly emailed the picture to the contact at the show, thinking, *The Black Sheep became the Superstar!*

CHAPTER 17

Post Paris Love

"You know, Susan, I think Kolton and Darla are going to get together at the wedding."

Shelly and I were at the Bobbi Brown counter testing eyeshadows and blush a few days before her big day. It was December and I had been asked to be a Scripture reader for the ceremony. Darla was a friend of the bride and a literature professor at my alma mater. Apparently she had met Kolton and like so many other women before me, had in the words of Jane Austen "grown to highly esteem him."

I asked Shelly if she was SURE Kolton liked Darla because I breezily mentioned I kind of liked him and I was excited to see him at the ceremony. She assured me they liked each other and then changed the subject stating I would be perfect with her soon-to-be husband's brother. "He's very sweet, lives in Hong Kong and has a house-keeper and a driver. He's got a great job."

It was as though she hadn't heard me.

"You really see me in *Hong Kong*?" I had been to

Hong Kong about a decade earlier. It was a fascinating city, but not a place I would dream about moving to. Too congested. Too foreign. In France I could decipher some of the street signs with my knowledge of Spanish. I had no knowledge of Chinese, the spoken language or the characters.

Shelly didn't budge, saying yes, she could see me there and Hong Kong was very cosmopolitan. I dropped the subject. It was apparent she was not my wingman.

For the wedding rehearsal, I wore a turquoise sweater set with sparkly beads trimming the neckline and sleeves and shiny gray pants from Banana Republic. My hair had been recently highlighted. I had a bit of a California tan. I was flashy and hoped to catch the eye of a certain violin maker.

I arrived at the church a few minutes late. The wedding party and family were already seated in the front pews reviewing details with the the pastor. I held my head up high and walked with a smile down the aisle to the front. Shelly turned and gave me a hug. I saw Kolton smile and nod from his seat in the pew. After greeting the bride and her family I made my way over to my dreamy friend who I hoped to make more than a friend.

"Hey, Kolton. Mind if I squeeze in next to you?" He leaned to the side so I could pass him in the narrow pew.

"Good to see you," he opened his arms, encircling me in a hug.

I wasn't sure who or where Darla was, but found it interesting she and Kolton weren't sitting together. Soon I figured out who she was when she came over to sit down on the other side of Kolton. Darla had a short dark bob and wore heavy dark clothes. Her face was colorless. We exchanged introductions and Darla began speaking in low tones to Kolton. I noticed the non-verbals. Kolton wasn't sitting straight in the pew, but his body position was slightly tilted toward my side. His leg was crossed and pointing my direction.

I asked Darla if she enjoyed teaching at my alma mater. I was trying to be the bigger person. Or at least I was trying to analyze my rival. She gave a hesitating answer that was condescending to my school. I got the sense it wasn't as academic as an institution as she would have fancied.

What could Kolton *possibly* see in her? She wasn't friendly. Or funny. At the end of the rehearsal she paraded over to the piano, sat down and started pounding out a dramatic concerto. I ignored her as did the rest of the party. We were engaged in conversation with each other. She kept playing, desperate, it seemed, for attention.

The wedding participants migrated to the lobby in preparation to leave for the rehearsal dinner and Kolton said, "I have something for you." He handed me a label that read "FRIEDLAND." I tilted my head and smirked.

"Remember when you were in Paris how my mailbox had the wrong name on it still? Not long after you left, I took down the name to put mine up and underneath the name that was there, was this name. I saw Friedland and I laughed out loud. I knew I had to show it to you."

He'd thought of me at least once since the Paris trip!

I gave him a hard time about making sure he took good care of MY apartment.

He brought me a label. A *label*. It must be love.

At the rehearsal dinner in a Chinese restaurant, Kolton sat across from me. We laughed and bantered, and I couldn't see any interest on his part toward the professor. But then I surmised maybe it was like when I had a crush on Ryan Rollins in high school speech class. I liked him so much I couldn't show it.

After the meal he walked with me to the car, my dad's brand new SUV with heated seats. He wanted to see the vehicle. I unlocked the doors and hopped in. He opened the passenger's side and looked around, admiring the interior. "Nice. Your dad picked a good car."

Pause.

"Maybe you could give me a ride back to Stephan's place."

"Oh. Is that where you're staying? Where is it again?" He told me where it was, and I informed him it was about 45 minutes out of the way of my parents' house, which was where I would be staying.

"Oh, that's kind of far," he observed.

"Yes. It is kind of far. Well, have a good night. I'll see you tomorrow at the wedding."

All the way home I was kicking myself. I had the opportunity for alone time in the car with the man I had a raging crush on and I choked. "Yes. It is kind of far." How stupid was I? It was a heck of a lot closer than Paris! I hoped Darla wasn't the one giving him a ride back to Stephans's.

The wedding the next day was lovely, and what made it even lovelier was the mix up in the reception seating. The wedding participants were supposed to walk through the door and be introduced, taking a seat at the head table. I was supposed to be seated next to the brother-in-law who lived in Hong Kong, and Kolton was supposed to be by the side of the professor. Instead, the professor was at the complete opposite end of the table glaring at me as Kolton and I ended up at one end together laughing and chatting throughout the dinner courses.

I tried very hard not to talk my crush's ear off. I sincerely felt there was an equal give and take in our conversation. It occurred to me if Kolton truly were interested in getting together with the professor, he sure was spending a lot of energy socializing with me. He could have excused himself to approach the professor and chat with her for a bit. People milled around, gregariously celebrating. Instead, he stayed in his seat by my side as we reminisced about our days in Paris and spoke of the comical minutiae of life.

As the dessert was served, Darla prowled over to a vacant seat on the opposite side of Kolton. "Hey guys. How are you doing? You look like you're having an interesting conversation."

I didn't like her at all, but I wasn't heartless. I greeted her warmly and asked how she was doing, engaging her in conversation. I observed how Kolton's body language was very indifferent toward her. I was more welcoming than he was. Was Shelly overstating this budding romance?

Following the dessert conversation, the DJ began to warm up the crowd for dancing. I remembered Kolton wasn't a dancer. I excused myself from "the couple" and made my way over to my date. That's right. I brought a date. I couldn't be perceived as having no prospects, and wouldn't a mysterious man by my side make Kolton a little more interested in me? My brother-in-law once that men like women that other men like. So I asked a guy friend who had been one of the students in the high school youth ministry I had led in college to be my date. It sounds worse than it was; he was 23 and I was 30. Besides, he was 6'7", so he wasn't a kid anymore. My wedding date was also my wingman. He made small talk with the random folks he was assigned to at the singles table.

"What do you think? Does Kolton like me or Darla?" I leaned in and kept my voice low.

"Well he talked to you long enough," he said, sounding a little irritated.

"Sorry. Are you having an okay time?"

"I'm fine. I got to cut the steak for the girl with her arm in a sling. That was exciting."

"You're such a good sport. Thanks. Hey, do you want to dance?"

"Sure. Why not," he said flatly.

We danced to a few songs and then took a break. The DJ announced, "Let's have the bride and groom on the dance floor. Bride and groom please." After Shelly and Stephan danced for a little while he started up again, "Now let's have all the married couples on the dance floor. All you married folks." A cluster of older people joined the newlyweds and swayed cheek to cheek around the floor.

After a bit, the DJ said, "Now, if you're not dancing and you see someone who you'd like to marry, ask him or her to dance." My heart sank when I saw Kolton, the non-dancer, approach Darla and they danced the rest of that song and the next. GRRR. I didn't dance with my date since in the back of my mind I knew he had at one point had a crush on me. I didn't want to lead him on to think ours would be the next wedding.

The brother-in-law from Hong Kong was nowhere to be seen. I passed him once on the way to the restroom and said a brief hello. The DJ played a few more standard wedding numbers. I danced out of obligation; I felt bad because there weren't many people on the dance floor, and I knew my friend's family had probably paid good money for the entertainment. After I'd been out there for a bit doing my good deed by groovin', a stormy looking Kolton suddenly appeared before me. "May I have this next dance?" I nodded and he took my hands.

"You are someone whose friendship I value. I hope we can keep communicating even though we're apart. I'm glad we've gotten to know each other." I nodded and agreed. I knew I was great at keeping in touch with friends. Especially if they were men and I thought they were hot. I danced out the rest of the song with him, not exactly understanding what seemed so urgent for him to share with me, but happy to have been asked to dance, even if he had danced with Darla too.

Something in his way of speaking, his intentionality in sharing the dance with me, made me know even though the powers that be may have been cheering on Darla, I had the upper hand.

When I hugged and said good-bye to Kolton at the wedding, I knew it wasn't really goodbye. In my heart I knew someday I'd see him again.

CHAPTER 18

Police Scene

ONE NIGHT I met my friend Dana, my fan from the horse show, at the Derby. It was a dance venue in Hollywood that was hopping thanks to the revival of the big band swing dance scene. I was looking forward to this night because she said several local church singles groups were going to be meeting there. I figured I could possibly happen upon a nice, mature, responsible guy and Charleston off into the sunset with him.

I was so eager to make it to the Derby to meet Mr. Right I got stopped by a police officer for making a late left turn on red onto Hillhurst, the street directly in front of the Derby. Turning left on red is okay if you're the first one hanging out in the intersection, but apparently it's not okay if you're the third car like I was. I'm not sure how the cop had the heart to ticket me since I looked so sweet and vintage with my hair in victory rolls and my lips adorned with bright red lipstick.

I tried to put the sting of the ticket aside and smiled as the doorman took my cash and stamped my hand. My eyes adjusted to the dark and Dana approached me. "Hey, Girlie!" She greeted me with a long drawn out "hey," a last vestige of her Southern accent. As we walked over to the bar right next to the dance floor I declared, "You won't believe what just happened. I got a $271 ticket for making a left turn on red," I moaned. I needed to drown my sorrows in a Diet Coke. I was going to live large and ask for a twist of lime.

"Oh! I'm sorry. That stinks. What happened?" I told her of my incident.

"Well, the way I look at it, think of all the times you *haven't* been caught and you were speeding. It's kind of like paying your dues. It's covering you for the times you weren't caught."

"You're right. But why is it $271? Such a weird amount." I tried to shake the bad vibes. Dana attempted to cheer me up by suggesting we dance.

We made our way to the large party room with the wooden floor. Music from the band in the bar area was piped in to that side of the establishment. Large screens in the background played black and white clips of old-time Hollywood dance movies. We stood there for a moment and surveyed the room. I recognized some people from dancing somewhat regularly at this swing dance venue— The Chatter, Fedora Man, and the guy who looked like he'd played in the NFL.

One new face stood out from the rest. He was dark and handsome, rather exotic looking like he was part Polynesian. He wore a red letterman's sweater and handsome smile. A magnetic air of confidence and sensuality flowed from his footwork to his face, and he was by far the best dancer in the room.

My reverie was interrupted when someone asked me to dance. I came back into the moment, temporarily forgetting my new crush as I rockstepped and twirled with my present partner. After a few more dances with various partners, my heart jolted when I turned around realizing red sweater guy was asking me to dance.

His name was Geoff, and he was even more charming in conversation than from a distance. We laughed and chatted and had a great dance. I thanked him and he thanked me. Later he asked me to dance again. After the song we stood at the side of the floor talking.

"I should get your number. I organize these swing nights and round up a bunch of people from my circle of friends, church, etc. I'll let you know the next time we have another big swing mixer."

I cheerfully gave him my number, amazed *the* hottest guy and best dancer spent a few minutes talking to me *and* wanted to include me on his call list for upcoming events.

I was even more thrilled when a couple of days later he called. "Hey, Susan. It's Geoff from the Derby. I really enjoyed meeting you the other night and it was fun talking to you. I'd like to take you out for a bite to eat or coffee and get to know you better." No beating around the bush. No, "let's hang out sometime." I couldn't stand that vague "hanging out" business many guys were prone to. Geoff was genuinely interested in me and was pursuing me. Hallelujah!

I met him at the Farmer's Market in Beverly Hills a few days later. We had meatball sandwiches at a mom and pop food stand. Things were going well, so we went to a movie. It was hideously boring, about some tragic event that happened on a submarine. I would have dozed off but couldn't since I was still in awe of Geoff. I dreamed of how good of a dancer I'd become if we started dating.

The film ended and we walked outside the theater. The outdoor mall area was a virtual ghost town. The lights were still on near the fountain and jasmine bloomed on the bushes nearby. Geoff snapped off a small white blooming branch of a fragrant flowers and extended them toward me. I smiled, thanked him and held it. Then he took it from me and placed it in my hair. Like a true gentleman he walked me to the parking garage to my car. When we got there it was obviously time to say goodnight but he was stalling.

I'm not sure how it happened, but he said he wanted to check my oil, and it wasn't a euphemism. He asked me if I ever checked my oil, and I told him I didn't since I had it changed every 3,000 miles. In a fatherly or older brotherly tone he explained, "You know, you really should learn how to check your oil. It's important it's at the right level and it's easy to do. May I pop the hood?" I found this whole scenario a bit odd, yet I started to think checking my oil every now and then was probably a good idea. I was entranced. I sheepishly admitted I wasn't really sure how to pop the hood, as I opened the driver's side door of my SUV and located the correct lever to release the hood.

Geoff could have been performing for a driver's ed video. He broke down every step in checking the oil and the reasons why it was so important. It seemed a little too complicated for me. I outwardly hung on every word, but inside was thinking, "I'll still just take it to Jiffy Lube. But keep talking; I like your company and I think you should kiss me."

He didn't.

My internal reverie was interrupted when I saw him grab a napkin from inside the slot of my opened door and wipe his hands off. I couldn't stop him in time and didn't have the heart to tell him on the way over I was hard pressed to find a Kleenex and so I had grabbed that napkin to blow my nose. He kept right on talking and didn't seem to notice anything unusual on his hands.

The night ended with a hug and I drove away thinking about how impressed my dad would be he had looked at my oil. I knew my mom would like him because he was so forthright about getting to know me. And, of course, I was in heaven. For once a hot guy I had interest in reciprocated interest. Maybe I had a future beyond being the single horse lady.

I saw Geoff one more time for dinner and he greeted me with a feathery kiss on the lips. We ate at an Argentinian restaurant and he held my hand in between courses. I was falling. Slight problem: I was going to be returning home to Chicago for the summer like I normally did after the long school year. I'd be away for two months. I told him this and he seemed okay with it. What a keeper!

The summer came and went. I had quality family time in Illinois, but was ready to return to L.A. in August and begin my swinging single life again. I contacted Geoff and heard back from him after a slightly delayed response of several days. He said we should get together soon but didn't mention an exact time. I was a little put out, but realized it might take a while to build back the momentum. Absence doesn't always make the heart grow fonder.

September rolled around and I was in Seattle at a wedding. I had about given up hope on seeing Geoff again, but then I got a call while at Anthropologie shopping with the other bridesmaids. He asked when I'd be back home and we set up a time to get together. He invited me to his apartment for dinner and a movie. He would make the dinner and I would bring the movie.

I drove to Santa Monica with my roller blades in the back of my car and butterflies in the bottom of my stomach. I hadn't seen Geoff in a few months, and I wondered if he was still interested in me or if we were just friends. I guessed by the end of the night I'd know for sure.

Geoff and I had a pre-dinner skate along the ocean. On the way over, I was hoping I wouldn't have to face any hills and I wouldn't have to stop since I didn't quite have the braking part figured out. I knew how to stop on rollerblades in theory, but it was a whole different story in practice. It usually involved running into a parked car or the side of a building. If it came down to it, I could always grab Geoff if I needed brakes. Maybe that wouldn't be so bad after all.

We bladed along the boardwalk and wound up at Muscle Beach, where it seems as though there's a beach party continually in progress. A giant boombox throbbed a baseline as people roller skated, skateboarded, bladed and played basketball along the water. Geoff, ever the show off, grabbed my hands and pulled me into closed position. We proceeded to swing skate to the music. I had never seen anything like it or done anything like it before. I'm not exactly the most demonstrative person and I don't like doing things where people can see me. However, that all changed with Geoff as my lead. I just went with it. Cheesy? Yes. Embarrassing? A little. He had enough confidence for the both of us, so I literally and figuratively rolled with it and pretended this is what I normally did on dates. Danced on rollerblades.

Before heading back to Geoff's, we stopped by the gymnastics equipment for which Muscle Beach is named. Geoff took off his skates and socks, ran up to the rings, grabbed them and began swinging. He twirled upside down and did handstands. He was a regular Bart Connor. "That takes a lot of upper body strength," he proclaimed after his performance.

We bladed back to Geoff's gated apartment complex. It was surprisingly nondescript on the outside but made up for it on the inside. Geoff had a female mannequin in his apartment. He was an artist, but I still thought it was creepy. He lived alone. At least that's what I thought.

Geoff went into the bathroom and freshened up a bit. He came back all smiley and smelled delicious. I used the bathroom next to wipe the shine off my nose and tend to my weathered ponytail.

I joined Geoff in his galley kitchen where he was in the middle of preparing salmon. We small talked and he told me how much he preferred staying in and cooking—you could eat so much healthier and cheaper as opposed to going out. It crossed my mind maybe he was trying to get off cheap on this date. We got our plates and plopped down on the sofa to watch the Woody Allen movie I had brought—*Everyone Says I Love You*—a campy musical.

About 15 minutes into the film the phone rang, and Geoff took the call into the other room. He came back out a minute or two later and then went over to his curtains and pulled them closed. He sat back down next to me and we finished our meal and then leaned back into the couch, shoulder to shoulder. I was waiting for him to try the ol' Greg Brady yawn trick, where the guy stretches his arms up and then slips one arm around the girl, when the phone rang a second time. Geoff jumped up and went into the other room again. This time he came back and let out a long sigh.

"Hey. Is everything okay?" I sensed something was wrong.

Geoff shook his head. "You remember my ex-girlfriend?" I nodded. He had told me I didn't hear from him for a few months because he had started seeing someone from his church. It was a short-lived relationship, and he was back on the market. "Well, she keeps calling me. I think she might be on her way over here."

I said he could just tell her he had company and was unable to see her. He didn't like my idea. I asked why she was coming over if he didn't invite her.

"She's very hard to persuade. I don't know what to do."

Geoff got up and paced back and forth across the room. I couldn't fathom why he was so upset. If the ex came over, he could let her in and she'd see he was entertaining someone else. As a result, she would be embarrassed and and leave.

At least that's how I would feel. But not her, I realized a few minutes later when Geoff's entrance gate was buzzed repeatedly.

Geoff slumped down onto the couch.

"Well, are you going to answer the door?" He shook his head.

The buzzing got more aggressive and became continuous.

"What are you going to do?"

Geoff whispered, "If you go on my balcony, you can easily climb over to the neighbor's balcony. Then I'll let her in and tell her to go away."

At this point I thought Geoff was out of his mind. "I'm not doing that!" I had nothing to hide. Why should I go climbing around?

I was so naïve.

The buzzing stopped for a minute and then the pounding on the door began.

"Geoff! I know you're in there. Just open up. I left my license in your apartment. I need my license. Open up and I'll get my license and leave. I promise." The ex had a husky New York accent that made her words seem all the more threatening.

My alarm mounted, "How'd she get in?"

Geoff whispered a neighbor must have let her in when they were leaving.

"Do you feel like you're being stalked?" Geoff nodded gravely.

"This is like *Fatal Attraction*. Why can't you just tell her to go away?"

"I know. I'm going to call my buddy Sam and ask him to talk some sense into her." That made very little sense to me—asking your friend to talk to your ex. So junior high!

I tried to continue watching the movie and Woody Allen's attempt to woo Julia Roberts while the pounding persisted and Geoff was in the kitchen on the phone with Sam. He came back and said, "I'm going to ask her to leave and I might use language I would be uncomfortable having you hear, so I'd like you to go into my bedroom and close the door."

I did as I was told—anything to get her to leave. As soon as I shut and locked the bedroom door thinking, "Great! This looks *real* good. Very innocent. I'm hiding in his bedroom," Geoff began shouting and cursing and demanding for her to leave. The ex screamed back and a thunderous pounding was followed by more screams. It sounded like a barroom brawl.

I panicked thinking, "What is going on out there?!? This is like a bad movie. And I'm in it! How did I get into this situation? I'm a schoolteacher. What if she busts down this door?" I was sure she was tougher than me because of her accent. Besides, I grew up in a family of all girls—we didn't fight—and I wasn't a natural athlete.

I hunted around Geoff's room for a baseball bat. I couldn't believe how outrageous this whole situation was. What would I even do with a bat? I breathed a sigh of relief when I remembered how buff Geoff was. I thought back to the date when we were out on my balcony and he puffed out his bulging pectorals and told me to touch his chest. I did and smiled and nodded in admiration.

If she comes in here and tries to hurt me, Geoff will kick her ass. He could totally take her.

Then I thought, *Wait! Geoff better not kick her ass. She's a girl. He'd better not put a hand on her.*

It was too late.

The shouting stopped but I stayed in the room. I was sure the neighbors could hear the pounding of my heart. Sirens blared and then stopped. Another tenant heard the pounding and ensuing fight. I continued to try to act normal in Geoff's bedroom. I wished I hadn't left my cell phone in my purse which was in the other room.

After what seemed like hours, I slowly opened the bedroom door and saw the front door on the floor, splinters strewn across the carpet. Geoff was sitting on the floor against the wall with his face in his hands. A police officer approached me and asked if I had witnessed what had just happened.

"Well, not exactly. I was in the other room." He led me into the kitchen, away from Geoff where he interviewed me. He asked a handful of official questions and then asked me unofficially how well I knew Geoff and hinted I probably shouldn't see him again. I asked where the girl was and he said she was in the police car—she was going to jail for breaking and entering. He said they probably should be taking Geoff in too because of the shape the girl was in, but they didn't want them in the same car together.

The police left and I popped the movie out of the VCR. Geoff offered to walk me to my car. We descended the stairs in silence.

"I bet you'll never want to see me again," Geoff broke the ice.

"Well, I don't know if I'd say it like that."

"I'll call you."

I said goodbye and I drove away, mulling over the intense and unfortunate date. How could that have been real? I thought he was a nice Christian guy, but his actions were not in alignment with What Would Jesus Do.

I didn't sleep well, and told my roommate the whole tale while we were getting ready for work the next morning.

"What?!?! Are you KIDDING me?! That's terrible. You're not going to see him again right?"

"I'm really attracted to him . . . I liked how proactive he was in getting to know me, but no. I can't see him."

Geoff called me during work hours the next day to ask me to prepare a statement for him to use in court. He said I had to just write down the facts. I thought I could do that; I said I'd see what I could come up with.

The last drop of compassion I had for my disaster date

dissolved when I got a phone call from a friend involved in a counseling ministry at her church. "There's a woman I spoke to who was beaten up pretty badly by her boyfriend. It's Geoff. I know you were there."

Apparently Geoff was in an "intimate, monogamous relationship" with this woman he had referred to as his ex! Unsure of what their actual relational status was on the night of our police-had-to-intervene date, I was furious this man had dragged me into his relational drama. I was also angry my friend had a moment of questioning my character when it became evident by naively going on a rollerblading, Woody Allen movie-watching date, I had become the other woman.

The next day during my conference period, I sat down at my computer and typed a letter outlining to Geoff that I did not want to hear from him again—ever. That I was NOT going to prepare a statement for his legal purposes and I thought he should see a counselor. I told him he was wrong to drag me into his relational dishonesty—it was not the kind of person I was. I scolded him for lying to me about his "ex-girlfriend."

The letter did the trick. I never heard from him again.

Sadly, I stopped going to the Derby. I had done nothing wrong, yet I felt like I couldn't face Geoff. If I happened to see him again with his flirtatious smile and puffed out chest, I thought I might use words I would be uncomfortable hearing myself say.

CHAPTER 19

California Visit

AFTER SHELLY'S WEDDING, Kolton and I kept in sporadic contact via email for the next few years. I moved on in terms of my affections, but I had a dormant crush on the violin maker. I was euphoric when I received an email stating Kolton was coming to Los Angeles to sell a few of his violins. I typed back an immediate response, saying I owed him at least a few days of hospitality considering his generosity in allowing me to stay with him in Paris.

He said he'd love to stay with me!

And so, the day after the dramatic police-involved date, I headed to LAX to pick up my European guest.

I noticed his hair had grown a bit longer and was a mop of brown waves. We hugged and made our way to the rental car counter. I asked if he was getting a convertible.

"No. I just rented the least expensive thing I could."

"Maybe we can sweet talk them into giving you a convertible. Let me try."

The rental agent was a man. I smiled, turned on the

charm, and urged the agent to offer us an upgrade "so our European visitor will have excellent memories of his stay in L.A."

The rental car rep apologized and said it really wasn't in his power to assign a free upgrade. I assured him I understood and my philosophy was that it never hurt to ask. He completed the paperwork and handed Kolton the keys. We walked out to the lot, and Kolton stopped short and laughed.

"Look! He gave me the convertible."

Kolton pointed to a silver Mitsubishi Spider. "That's unbelievable. That would never happen in Germany."

"Well, what'd I tell you? California is the promised land."

Over the next few days, Kolton became a fixture on the blow-up mattress in the living room. I went to work, he made his violin rounds in L.A. In the evenings we went out. One night to Santa Monica (in the convertible), on another night to a small Italian restaurant. I was falling for him . . . again.

At one point during our time together I casually asked about Darla. "I heard you two were going to get together. Whatever became of that?"

He offered up some simple story about how he had tried to have a relationship with her and went to see her for a weekend in Chicago, but he couldn't go through with it. He said he had a nice time, but when he got back home in Europe, he realized he didn't want to be in a relationship with her.

"We didn't have enough of a connection."

Vindicated! I thought. I knew it all along! I could tell from his body language during Shelly's wedding.

The last day of Kolton's stay came, and I drove him to Pacific Palisades so he could see friends of his who had been missionaries in Europe. They were going to entertain him for a few days. I was curious to find out how a missionary family could afford to live in Pacific Palisades.

As we cruised down the 101 freeway toward our ocean-side destination, Kolton told me he was very attracted to assertive women. His first girlfriend in Germany apparently won him by walking over to him at a party, sitting on his lap and giving him a kiss. Was he trying to send me a message, or just sharing a vignette from his teens?

We made it to the house in the Palisades and I was ready to say goodbye and skedaddle. I couldn't handle the tension anymore. Kolton asked me to come in to meet his gray-haired friend. The man asked me if I had time to come in for tea. How could I refuse?

So Kolton, the middle-aged missionary and I had tea, during which the host asked if we'd like to go on a little hike and see a beautiful view of the ocean. I said it sounded lovely, meanwhile I was trying to read Kolton to see if he was anxious to be rid of me. I excused myself to the powder room to take care of personal business before our "hike," which the host assured me was basically a walk up the hill of their street. The phone rang as I was re-entering the room, and with that the plot changed. The formerly cheerful man wore a look of concern.

"My wife's stranded down at the market. Her car

won't start. Do you two think you could drive me over there so I can help her?" I said I had nowhere to be. Good for me. More time with Kolton!

A couple of hours later after I had met the wife and jumped her new car that wouldn't start, I was in the kitchen of the missionary's home being asked to help cut tomatoes for our dinner. I had been invited to join Kolton and the family. They didn't want to send me home with an empty stomach since I had in a sense "saved" the wife by dropping her husband off to help her. He was able to get a tow to a mechanic's shop.

I chopped with care and precision, hoping Kolton wouldn't notice my lack of domesticity. Did each section of tomato have to be uniform? Our hostess seemed agitated, I assumed from her car trouble. She said her son had just had similar car problems out near Joshua Tree National Forest a few hours earlier. She made a subtle comment about the cars not working, insinuating it was due to spiritual warfare. That caught my attention.

Although our hostess seemed distracted over the family's car woes, she effervescently offered Kolton and me a water to sip while we waited for dinner. While she was bustling around the kitchen, I asked Kolton if she was okay, and he said her personality was kind of like that— busy and nervous.

A few minutes later after Kolton and I had made ourselves comfortable sitting on a sofa across the room from the kitchen, the phone rang. Kolton said to me in a hushed tone, "Well I hope nobody died." I'm sure he was thinking that the previous phone calls received all had to do with some kind of family emergency.

A few seconds into the phone conversation we heard, "Oh. Really. Oh no. That's too bad," Kolton and I exchanged glances. Our hostess got off the phone, "Well that's pretty sad. My uncle just died."

I am not proud of what transpired next. I know the death of someone's loved one is not a laughing matter, but it was a combination of all the day's fiascos along with the seemingly harmless comment by Kolton hoping no one had died and then the wild-eyed look of disbelief and horror on Kolton's face when he realized someone had indeed died, that made me do a most unladylike, impolite thing. I simultaneously laughed and stifled the laughter and sprayed my sip of water I had just gulped back into my cup. Thank God it was an opaque gold cup.

The announcement was too much for me to take and I literally leaped off the couch and veered into the darkened hallway where I doubled over in silent laughter. I couldn't breathe. I knew I was wrong, but I just couldn't help it. I hoped the bereaved hostess didn't notice.

After a few minutes of trying to compose myself in the hallway by forcing deep breaths and focusing on the seriousness of the situation, I nonchalantly walked back in and sat down next to Kolton. I felt less guilty when I heard the uncle was a much older man who had lived a very long, full life. His time was up on this earth and he went to be with his Lord.

The rest of the meal went swimmingly, and I met the formerly stranded son who had been at Joshua Tree when he made it home for dinner. He was a model. Not bad company. I had a violin maker on one side and a model on the other as I dined in Pacific Palisades.

Darkness fell over the Southland, and it was time for me to leave. I felt at this point Kolton was like family. Or at least I could see us having one, with little blond bilingual kids who played the violin. We had the same humor (at the expense of a dead uncle) and we seemed to enjoy each other's company, and he was not interested in Darla.

We hugged and said goodbye. One more time.

PART V

Show Season

CHAPTER 20

You'll Just Know

"IT'S GORGEOUS, RHONDA. You will be a stunning bride."

I was seated on a plush ottoman in the fitting room of the bridal department of Marshall Field's on State Street. My sweet college friend glowed in her ivory dress as she posed in front of the mirror. My stomach churned and my hands felt damp. I hoped it would go away before my blind date in a few hours.

It was April of 2004. Spring break, to be exact and I was in Chicago visiting family. I was fortunate enough to be in town at the same time Rhonda was picking up her gown for her August wedding. She was marrying a man I met through swing dancing a few years earlier. As Rhonda and I drove north on Lake Shore Drive, sleek skyscrapers on the left, Lake Michigan on the right I confessed, "I'm really, really nervous about this date. Like sick to my stomach nervous."

"Really? Why do you think that is? You've been on first dates before. It's not that big of a deal."

"I know, but I think I'm going to *really* like this one."

Shane was a super cute guy I met online during the dawn of Internet dating who lived in Chicago and worked for a university. He was scheduled to come to my friend's apartment and pick me up for our date.

Shane sent me an innocuous email commenting on some aspect of my dating profile. Most of the men who contacted me were much older men (as in almost my dad's age) or in foreign countries and whose motives I questioned. When I saw his picture attached to his intro message, he seemed so normal and friendly.

I knew this one had potential. Not only was he my physical ideal (tall, dark and handsome) but he was well-read, well-traveled, and even had a dog! And the fact he grew up on a farm in upstate New York was the icing on the cake, as I've always been drawn to people with an agricultural bent.

A few hours later when the buzzer of Rhonda's apartment sounded, I looked at her frantically. "What should I do? I need water!" My mouth was cottony and my heart raced. Rhonda assured me I should sit and relax. She would answer the door since it was her place.

Sit and relax?

Rhonda was so calm and collected. I thought maybe she should go along on the date too.

"Susan, Shane's here," Rhonda called out as if I didn't know. I walked over to the open door and time stood still.

His online profile picture was completely accurate. At the threshold stood a tall, athletic looking man with a kind, all-American face with light freckles. His straight brown hair both spiked up and pointed down in different places. He was fashionable without seeming metrosexual.

I shook his hand, not knowing if I was too professional or not ladylike enough. In the back of my mind I thought, "I get it now. He's the one."

Some married people talk about how when they first met their beloved, they immediately knew he or she was "the one." When pressed, they never explain how, instead offering, "When it happens to you, you'll just know."

Now I knew.

After drinks and chatting with Rhonda in her living room, Shane and I journeyed off on our own, commencing our date. I felt so alive strolling down the sidewalk with such an interesting, attractive man by my side. The blustery, barely spring air along with his company awakened my senses.

After dinner he took me to a hipster coffeehouse and then on to a family-owned ice cream parlor In operation since the 1920s. We sat in the same booth the Beatles sat in when they were guests there decades before. Three destinations in three separate neighborhoods of Chicago in one night seemed like a good sign. I left for L.A. with the hope of a budding romance.

After a few more phone calls, daily email exchanges and a weekend invitation to Chicago to see a band he knew play at the House of Blues, I was convinced Shane was intentional about forging a relationship. I suspected he was "in." This was exciting! I didn't really see myself as the kind of person who flew halfway across the country to spend a weekend with a guy I had only been out with once, but I had a good feeling.

Upon arriving in Chicago, he gave me a gift bag containing tea and a mug from the coffeehouse where we had our first date. That weekend we packed in the concert, a trip to the Field Museum, many long walks with his dog, ate hot dogs in the car at the iconic Superdawg, watched DVDs at his apartment, and even though it was a good 20-minute drive from his neighborhood, he ordered pizza from Lou Malnati's, my favorite pizza place in the world.

We said goodbye at O'Hare, and I was confident I'd receive a parting kiss. Not so. However, I knew he liked me. I figured he was a good old-fashioned, take-it-slow Christian guy.

A couple of weeks after my trip, Shane mentioned he had a plane ticket he had to use or lose. He had never been to California and asked if I would introduce him to the sights, sounds, and flavors of L.A. He scheduled a flight and told me he had a surprise he would reveal when he saw me in person. My curiosity was in overdrive.

The surprise was because he knew how much I loved to swing dance, he had been taking private dance lessons at an Arthur Murray studio in Chicago. He might not have shown his affection physically or verbally, but a guy making the effort to take *private dance lessons* for a girl was monumental. We went swing dancing together his first night in town. He was tentative dancing as many new leads are, but I thought he was brave to give it a shot. It was very flattering to think he went to such efforts to learn something I loved so we could enjoy it together. This was the stuff of which romance movies were made.

I asked Shane the next day if he'd like to explore Monterey and Carmel, explaining it was a really beautiful area and I had some friends from college who were like family with whom we could stay.

Shane was game to take a road trip and Ross, a dear friend from my college days and his family were up North and in town. We made the 5-hour drive and met our host in his Ralph Lauren-inspired tan and safari themed home. I got the guest room and Shane the couch.

The next day we went kayaking in Monterey Bay, then seafood dinner, and the following day we toured the Monterey Bay Aquarium and had Sunday brunch with Ross's family. A moment of awkwardness hung over the table when the Nicole, Ross's sister inquired, "So, how long have you two been dating?"

Shane seemed taken aback. He mumbled something about how long we'd been friends.

I thought, "I'm your FRIEND?!? That's all?" but played it off coolly.

Back at Ross's house, I asked Ross his opinion on the friend comment. He stated Shane seemed like a nice guy and it seemed like we enjoyed each other's company.

"But can you tell if he *likes* me?" I prodded. "I mean he wouldn't fly out here and take private dance lessons and email me every day and give me little gifts unless he liked me, right? He hasn't even tried to kiss me." Ross had no other insights.

At the end of the weekend, Shane and I headed back to L.A., driving down the scenic zig zags of Highway 101. We stopped along the way to snap photos of a beach filled with sea lions, gaze at the beauty of the rugged coastline, and have a snack at a quaint bakery. The trip had all the potential for a breakthrough romantic moment—holding hands in the car, a kiss on the beach. Yet nothing happened. My romantic weekend evolved into what seemed to be a platonic field trip, but I assured myself Shane was being very careful and a gentleman. He was sleeping on my couch after all.

Back in Pasadena we had one day left together. Shane opted to get a rental car so I wouldn't have to miss work the next day to drop him off at the airport. Somehow he ended up with a convertible. Which was great—especially for our final night's trip to Hollywood. Shane wanted to see the Chinese theater and the Walk of Fame. We drove with the top down and the heater blasting to alleviate the chill from the penetrating night air. In Hollywood we got out to examine some of the famed sidewalk stars and then returned to the car to head back; it was short and sweet visit. This trip to Hollywood was so much more promising than the one with my blind date from years before— the one where the police required me to drive my lapsed-licensed date home. As Shane turned the car toward home, he put in a CD, glanced my way and quietly said, "This song's for you."

Was this *the* moment? I had no idea who Nick Cave was, but the lyrics he intoned were, "Thank you girl, thank you girl, I will love you until the end of the world."

The moment we first met face to face back at Rhonda's apartment a couple of months earlier flashed before me. How he crossed the threshold and I somehow felt like

I already knew him, like I was re-meeting a long-lost friend.

After 33 years filled with dozens of lackluster dates, a few over-the-top fiascos, and a handful of painful unrequited love scenarios, I had finally met my Mr. Right.

Right?

CHAPTER 21

The Big Reveal

THREE WEEKS AFTER I bid Shane adieu following the Nick Cave serenade in L.A., I greeted him on a muggy night at Ogilvie Train Station in downtown Chicago. I had returned home to Illinois to spend the summer with my family, as was my custom. Shane lived only an hour away from my parents. He did not have reliable transportation; his teenage white SUV was on its last leg, but that was okay. I had a car and I lots of time on my hands.

I was sad to leave DC for the entire summer, as summer is meant for riding, but I was thrilled my horse was being ridden by a daughter of a friend who was very skilled with horses and who had a background in gymkhana and jumping. My first love would be in good equestrian hands for summer break, and I had to see what would become of "us."

I began volunteer teaching ESL to immigrant children from Africa. I viewed it as not only a way to serve, but also make friends in Chicago, as I had a suspicion my future might be leading me back there.

Twice a week after my Chicago tutoring gig, Shane and I would hang out from afternoon to evening. Some days we'd take his Lab mix to a dog park or simply stroll through his northside neighborhood of brick four-story apartment buildings from the Jazz Age. Some nights he would make dinner at his place; other nights we'd go to an outdoor café for dinner. It reminded me of Paris, minus the French.

On weekends we'd see each other at least once and take in a movie or go to a park. I faithfully traveled the 80 miles round trip to see my love interest. The commute didn't bother me, as I knew there wasn't much to do where my parents lived.

As Shane and I settled into a comfortable summer routine, I could envision this as a future lifestyle we would share. The apartment, the dog, the long walks, conversations about matters of justice, faith, or art. I was smitten.

"Haircut Day" was the one time Shane traveled out to my parents' home. My older sister Linda had started growing out her hair so she could donate it to Locks of Love, and I figured my hair was the same color as Linda's, so together we could help the nonprofit create one thick strawberry blonde wig. Shane gallantly offered to accompany me to the salon so I didn't have to walk the haircut journey alone.

My mom served lunch and doted on us by baking fresh peach cobbler from southern Illinois peaches. Peach season and sweet corn season are the pinnacle of summer glory for my dad. Some people count down until the NFL season starts—my family counts down to when sweet corn is sweetest and when southern Illinois peaches are ripe and ready.

It was strange—the longer my hair grew (and especially when I highlighted it so it seemed a little more blonde and a little less strawberry and wore it straight), the more the male species seemed to perk up in my presence. I would miss my feminine tresses, but it didn't matter. I was sure Shane liked me for who I was, not for something superficial like my long hair. Besides, I loved having a bob. So easy to style and very Gatsby-esque.

We arrived at the hair salon to see my mom's stylist. I got the time wrong and we ended up arriving an hour early. So, we headed to a coffee shop next door. It was there I revealed my secret to Shane.

With heart pounding and words tiptoeing out of my mouth in slow motion with lots of breath in between, I told Shane I had made a decision.

"This is not about you, but it's not *not* about you. There's a job fair for Chicago Public Schools next week and I'm going to it. I'd like to move back here to Illinois."

I had been dreaming of returning to my roots and returning my horse to the green fields of the Midwest once again where he could graze with a herd. So this wasn't entirely a wild, crush-induced plan.

Shane's eyes enlarged, then he smiled as though he just opened a longed-for Christmas present. We talked about the possibilities, and then it was time for my long ponytail to be snipped. I gave up 10 inches of hair and my secret future plan almost simultaneously.

What Shane didn't know was that a year earlier, I had actually attended a Chicago Public Schools job fair held at McCormick Place. I was prompted to seek a job in Illinois because I had been encountering soul restlessness. I'd kind of had it with California. It was a fun place to live, but not exactly the kind of place where I was meeting men who shared my values. My girlfriends were starting to marry and it seemed as if there was more of a future for me in Chicago. And if not a future, at least I could reconnect with my past. If I wasn't going to get married and have children of my own, I could be near my nieces and nephews and pour into them.

Maybe the loose ends of my life would align and I would have a reason to move back to Illinois.

CHAPTER 22

Settlers Settles It

SHANE AND I continued to see each other that summer and we did go swing dancing—once. He just wasn't comfortable enough with being uncomfortable on the journey to learn how to dance. Just like riding a horse is the only way to improve your riding skills, dancing is the only way to improve your dancing skills. None of my encouragement or coaxing seemed to have a positive effect; it just wasn't his thing. At least he had tried. Even though he stopped dancing with me after two tries, taking the surprise Arthur Murray lessons that spring was a still lovely gesture I was sure meant our relationship was something special with a future.

In addition to swing dancing, being on time wasn't really Shane's thing either. I shrugged off his lack of punctuality. It was summer! I had nowhere urgent to be and he did communicate with me when he was going to be late. Sadly, because of his lack of a reliable car and his indecision about dressing himself, I arrived late to Rachel's wedding.

When I arrived at his apartment after driving an hour into Chicago to pick him up, Shane had two different shirt and tie combinations laid out on his bed. I told him which one I thought looked nice and he threw them on. We then proceeded on to Lake Shore Drive to head south to the suburb where the wedding was taking place. It was a midsummer Saturday in Chicago. It seemed as though the whole city was also heading south on the city's main north-south artery. Then there was a huge traffic jam due to an accident.

What should have been an hour trip by car turned into almost two hours. I thought we could at least sneak in the back of the church. However, there is no sneaking in when your friend gets married in a small country chapel. We were late and it was painfully obvious. Instead of being light hearted because it was the day they were beginning their new life together, the bride and groom were extremely hurt by my being late, as I was supposed to bring them a video camera to record the ceremony.

The faux pas of our wedding lateness lingered, damaging my friendship with both bride and groom. My relationship with the couple never completely recovered.

However sad I felt about the cringe-worthy wedding tardy, my regret was partially assuaged when I was offered a job teaching at a brand new math and science charter school set to open on the north side of Chicago. Of my efforts standing in long Disneyland lines to sell myself to various school principals during a job fair, the one school that offered me a job at was located in Shane's exact neighborhood! The city of Chicago has over 200 neighborhoods in over 200 square miles yet, it was a few blocks from his home.

I accepted the sixth grade English position and Shane began to help me apartment and furniture hunt in earnest. He was actually looking for an apartment too; he had a roommate in line and the two of them could afford an upgraded place with the combined income. They found a recently renovated condo overlooking the park and the lake. Shane gave me a lead on an apartment he wanted until he saw the condo. I moved into the beautifully landscaped Tudor building and lived five blocks away from my crush/possible boyfriend on the same street!

I flew back to California to say my goodbyes, pack boxes and arrange to have DC shipped to Illinois. My horse would return to pastures and country living, and I would begin my new job adventure. The new school was two blocks away from my new place meaning I could walk to work! All the people I met at the school were young and vibrant, and most of them Turkish and male. I thought it a bit odd, but I didn't question it.

For my 33rd birthday in October, Shane revealed he had something special planned to celebrate. He took me first to dinner at a French restaurant and then back to the original coffeehouse we visited on our first date. There was a section where pillows were strewn about in a corner in the window overlooking the street, which had an Arabian vibe. I took advantage of the pillowy casualness and attempted to snuggle in close to Shane's side. We had a server take our picture and as soon as it was over, Shane quickly removed his arm from my shoulder.

I didn't understand the mixed messages. It seemed as though a French restaurant might lead to a French kiss, not a hurriedly removed arm around the shoulder.

I was perturbed and mentioned it to him as we sat on my couch later that evening, "You know as a woman turning 33 there are certain things in life that become important. For me, family is a priority and I hope to have my own someday. I don't know what you're looking for, but I hope 'this,' whatever this is we have, is building toward a future." I delivered my rehearsed lines that my sister helped me come up with.

Shane looked stunned by my directness and gave an almost whispered response of few words indicating he cared about me, but he was not sure about the future.

"This is not an ultimatum, but a request to think about it and to come to a conclusion. I am worthy to be more than a friend to you."

My girlfriends, who faithfully listened to every detail of my relationship, surmised Shane was a slow-moving, old-fashioned Christian guy. He was taking his time and that was respectable.

Two weeks after my birthday, Shane invited me over to meet his friends, a married couple, who were in town. He knew from his time at seminary. He was going to make dinner and he wanted me to join them for food and frivolity. My heart danced!

If he was inviting me to have dinner with a couple, it meant we were a couple. That's what couples did—they had dinner with other couples! It was dark and I drove to his apartment even though it was only a few blocks away.

Our neighborhood was sketchy in places—there was occasionally some gang activity, and a guy had been mugged near the El's Red Line stop a few blocks away, and I didn't want to be out late walking at night alone.

His friends seemed very sweet. They were also in their early 30s and had been married a few years. Shane made a curry dish with coconut milk. There are very few foods I don't like, but coconut is one of them, and I thought he knew it. I suddenly felt a bit less special. As dinner was being prepared the husband asked, "So how do you know each other?"

Shane replied, "We kind of met through a mutual friend."

What?!?! I thought incredulously. *The dating website is a person?*

"That's not really the case. We actually met online. I'm sure he can tell you more about that later, after I've left."

Shane looked as though he swallowed moldy food.

I was angry, but I held it together because I did understand how some people thought only crazies met people on Internet sites. If his friends were from the Bible Belt South, they were probably conservative and might think a dating site outlandish.

After dinner we played Settlers of Catan, a strategy game I had heard about for years. It was a favorite of my friend Ross. Once the game was underway, I completely understood why, and mentioned quietly to Shane, "This is Ross's favorite game."

"Ross! We know all about Ross," the wife exclaimed.

"Ross? They know all about Ross but they don't know about me? That's ridiculous!" I blurted. I was disgusted, but the game was near the end and I was winning. We played a bit longer and then I announced I had to go home. After exchanging "nice meeting you's," Shane walked me to my car as he simultaneously took his dog out one last time for the night.

We walked down the sidewalk in silence in the dark. After crossing the street to my car's parallel parking spot, I finally looked up at Shane. He was wearing a green parka with the hood up. The night wasn't the only thing cold on that street.

I paused. There was a hint of streetlight. This deserted city corner was not a place to stand around talking for long.

"Shane, I don't know what all happened back there. You lie to your friends about how we met? You can't tell them you were on an online dating site? You refer to me as a friend? I don't really understand what's so awkward about calling me your girlfriend! Lots of guys date and refer to the girl as their girlfriend. We're spending all this time together and it's really just a friendship? I don't need more friends—I already have a lot of those."

I then delivered the ultimatum.

"This phony relationship is over. Don't call me, and your Lab mix is ugly and looks more like a pitbull than a Lab, FYI." That's what I should have said. But ultimatums were uncharted territory for me and I still cared about him so much, even while livid.

What I actually said was, "Figure this out. And you

have a month to do so."

A month? Was that the right amount of time? Maybe too long.

My anger didn't leave room for heartbrokenness. And besides, in the movies when the girl gives the "straighten out your stuff" speech, the guy always comes around. I wasn't too worried.

I didn't call Shane. I knew he had to travel for his job and would be gone a few days. That worked for me. Plan "Cold Shoulder" was activated—for about three days.

When Shane came back to town he called me, leaving a benign voice mail: *Hi, how are you doing?*

I took the bait.

I dialed his number, and when we spoke on the phone my cold shoulder began to thaw. He *did* care about me. He wouldn't call me if he didn't want me in his life.

And so began another round of our not-dating dating.

I did want to stick to my word regarding the month ultimatum, but when I plotted it out on my calendar, the date the ultimatum was to go into effect was the day before his birthday. I couldn't do that to him. He took me to a French restaurant for my birthday a month earlier, so I had to do something. Probably something less overtly romantic, but something nice to reciprocate. I wanted to stand my ground, but I didn't want to be mean.

And so I took him to a riverboat casino for his birthday. He had never been to a casino. Not that a casino is an amazing birthday destination, but my choice was creative. He would have to respect my unique birthday plan.

The following week was Thanksgiving. Shane's parents lived out of state and he would not be celebrating with anyone. My mom and dad, sister and her family were planning to come to the city to have Thanksgiving at my apartment. I felt like a full-fledged adult—hosting a major holiday. Since Shane lived just a few blocks away and had nowhere to go I justified inviting him.

And so he came, bearing a yam side dish. We ate the meal without much fanfare. Shane seemed quiet and my family loud. Soon after the meal he excused himself. My family left shortly thereafter because they did not want to get caught up in expressway traffic. I was alone for Thanksgiving evening.

I kept thinking about the ultimatum and felt it was too late to enforce as the two of us kept functioning in a friendship-yet-maybe-more role. Besides, my new job was emotionally draining, and the last thing I needed was to add to my to-do list "break up with non-boyfriend." Life was complicated enough. The barn was my refuge, but it was so far away from my apartment, and school got out at 4:30 so I couldn't easily ride during the week. I didn't have any friends in my new neighborhood. The reality of living back in Illinois was not turning out as I'd hoped. Things hadn't yet fallen into place, so this relationship had to work because there was so much promise. And if it didn't, I would be really alone.

If Shane didn't like me, he wouldn't have wanted to spend a major family holiday with me. Maybe I needed to wait it out a little longer.

I mused his passion was of the slow-blooming variety,

and continued to wait for him to confess his affection and wrap me in his arms.

Christmas was approaching, and Shane thought he had a professional dog sitter lined up for his two-week vacation, but somehow I ended up dog sitting. I welcomed the chance to tangibly show my affection through service. I rationalized my actions because getting a dog was something I had contemplated, so I viewed this as a good test to see if becoming a dog owner was really up my alley. I went over to Shane's apartment to pick up the dog and was excited to give him his much-thought-about-before-purchased Christmas present, *The Slow Food Guide to Chicago*. I got a Starbucks thermos still in the Starbucks bag.

It was a letdown; I was hoping for something much more personal, but I overlooked it by figuring guys are clueless, and to him it probably was personal—he knew I liked coffee. Also, he *was* in a rush to get ready to leave for the holiday.

My cat was not keen on having a new roommate, but Shane's dog was a fine addition. I experienced the rhythm of three daily walks and twice daily feeding and all the tail wagging and playing in between. Having his dog for the holidays showed me this was not just something I could get used to, but grow to love. It felt so "me."

Shane came back to Chicago for New Year's Eve but he did not suggest getting together. He must have had jet lag. I went out to dinner with a few girlfriends and had a rather quiet evening. I respected Shane's need for personal space and I loved hanging out with the girls. A quiet welcome to 2005 was okay with me. I had something even better than a recently-opened Christmas present lined up—I was going to get my own dog! No worries about being the single cat lady—I was going to be the single horse/cat/dog lady, which had much less of a stigma.

CHAPTER 23

Walk This Way

THE FIRST TIME I took my dog Winnie for a walk, she took me for a walk. The phrase "drunken sailor" came to mind as my potential adoptee from the Doberman rescue organization zig-zagged several strides ahead of me sniffling scintillating scents on the crispy, faded January grass.

While I was being towed along to the right and to the left, in the street, up the sidewalk, and over by the mailbox post, I prayed the foster family's neighbors weren't looking outside their windows on their suburban street. I felt like the unfortunate star of a cartoon featuring a floppy-eared Doberman, nose to the ground, dragging a tall woman whose hair and scarf were flying out behind like a flag. I swear my body was at a 45-degree angle. I asked myself what I was getting into, as this kind of dog walk was anything but fun.

A moment earlier during my "meet the dog" appointment, Winnie's kind-hearted foster mom handed me a brown leather leash and told me to try her out—take the dog for a test drive. I assented, bundling up into my puffy winter coat, grabbing the leash like I knew exactly what I was doing. The show dogs I had seen on Animal Planet and the local hounds ambling nonchalantly alongside their owners in my neighborhood didn't do what my soon-to-be-dog was doing. Man was she strong.

Apprehension gripped me when I brought my new dog home; I was a little bit worried about inexperience with dogs and the inconvenience of the countless walks in store for me as dog owner living in a third floor apartment. I soon discovered walking my new dog was surprisingly like leading a headstrong horse. This was familiar territory since I had many years of experience with my Kentucky Thoroughbred. When Winnie, nose to the ground, ran ahead of me I instinctively blurted out, "Whoa!" instead of, "Heel!" I noticed too when I tried to get her to catch up to me when she was lagging behind due to an interesting aroma on the ground near the sidewalk, I would make the clucking sound that tells a horse to move faster. Was anyone watching this?

In addition to not wanting to be dragged, I dreaded one other thing about the walks. The "number two." I had cleaned many a litter box and mucked out many a stall, but something about picking up dog doo doo with a plastic grocery store bag made me want to simultaneously stop breathing, shudder, and wash my hands. I had recently gained experience with this hideous task when I dog sat for Shane.

For some reason, Winnie did not poop for the first two days I had her. It made me feel constipated and became the subject of a couple of anxious emails to the foster mom and the rescue agency representative who did my home visit.

My Doberman contacts said to hang in there and Winnie would soon adapt. One of them even mentioned I could try an old dog show trick if I got really desperate. She said to take a matchstick and stick it up my dog's butt and that would stimulate her system and she'd poop. The email said, "I probably don't even need to say this, but of course, it's an unlit match. And for obvious reasons, you probably want to do it when no one else is looking." I didn't take this piece of advice and it was okay. Winnie eventually did her business. I gave the update to her foster mom.

Hi Lynn,

Winnie's fitting right in.

The cat can't stand her (I'm not surprised— after all it's HIS apartment), but she keeps away. She walked into the place, went around all the rooms and then plopped down on her bed.

She didn't eat much last night or this a.m. She didn't go to the bathroom at all yesterday (I was a little worried). I took her for an early walk this a.m. and she did potty (off leash) when I let her loose on a tennis court.

Then I took her to my boyfriend's apartment. She met his dog and they hit it off. However, she POOPED in Shane's kitchen! I couldn't believe it.

We took the dogs for a walk and there's a fenced-in baseball field where we stopped. The two dogs play and played and played. It was fun to watch. Anyway, Winnie went #1 and #2 too, but I'm a little apprehensive she's not going to do it while on the leash.

I got her a jacket (kind of like a horse blanket) today.

Every new person she's encountered she's been very sweet to. In fact, Shane took to her immediately. He said today, "She's the kind of dog I wanted. You've got MY dog. One that likes to play, but can be MELLOW inside."

All that to say, I love her. She's my buddy. Thank you for everything.

Susan

I wasn't sure if I should use the word "boyfriend" to describe Shane, but there really was no better descriptor. Besides, it was too long of a story to really explain what we were to each other. And I didn't even really know.

Aside from those initial embarrassing walks, I discovered my dog was an eager learner and very smart. She knew the basics such as sit, shake, and stay. I had learned those from being around other dogs such as my aunt and uncle's Rascal, a black poodle who was thoughtful enough to buy, wrap, and write his name on a Christmas present for me every year when I was a little girl.

Being a teacher, it only made sense for me enroll my new dog in school. Maybe I could teach my dog some new tricks, or as it turned out, she would teach me some. We attended a beginning obedience class at Petsmart. There were no single guys there, but Winnie had a crush on a white male toy poodle. I told her she was so out of his league.

Meanwhile, this was exactly the same message my sisters and girlfriends were trying to communicate to me regarding Shane.

CHAPTER 24

Emancipation

SOMETHING MONUMENTAL OCCURRED three weeks into the new year as I was driving home from the barn on a Sunday. It was a bright, white winter afternoon and I had driven the 50 miles to ride DC. Thank God for indoor arenas. Winter was not my favorite season to ride in the Midwest. The bridle felt like cardboard and I had to warm up the cold bit in my hands before I could put it in DC's tender mouth. I hadn't figured out yet it was easy to put the bridle in the heated barn office while I was grooming and saddling up my horse.

Ross called. We'd catch up every couple of months via phone or text.

"How are things going with you and Shane?" I responded nothing had really changed much. Ross knew of the unsettling Settlers game and the "Oh, Ross, we've heard about him" comment. I said quickly I thought Shane liked me or he would stop coming around.

"Suz, if it hasn't happened yet, it's not going to happen. I think you need to date other people."

"But I don't even really *know* any other people. I live in the 'hood and I work a long day. All the men at work are married or Muslim. I don't want to go to bars. I've tried swing dancing and the scene here is very small and older. There's no one at church."

He tried to tell me none of that mattered, and I just needed to get out more and meet people and widen my social circle. I knew it was easier said than done. I found Chicago, "my" city, to be way more cliquey and closed off than California. When I had attended swing dances alone, I would only get asked to dance a few times, as opposed to in L.A., where I would rarely sit down the whole night. I tried finding new friends through my church, but it seemed I was either too old—I didn't connect well with the recent college graduates, or most of the people my age were married with young kids and lacked a need to expand their social circles.

I wondered if the six months of gray, unending winter translated to a universal dour mood of the city's inhabitants. Or was it just L.A. was a more transient city with people moving there from all over to burst into the entertainment world? A city with a large population of newcomers was more welcoming, as the newcomers were looking for new friends.

I protested that Shane and I were meant to be together. We had so much in common—except for punctuality—and it was just too weird out of *all* the neighborhoods in the city, I wound up in his backyard. It surely seemed as though God were orchestrating events to bring us together.

"Maybe so, but I think you need to see other people. And tell him." The last 10 minutes of this conversation occurred in my parked Jeep outside my apartment. I climbed the three flights of stairs to the wagging tail of Winnie and a meow from my cat.

I knew deep down Ross was right, so I decided to go back online to see if there were any new guys in the Chicagoland area I could potentially meet. I could take matters into my own hands and put myself out there.

I settled into my black office chair and logged into the website where I had met Shane, and to my horror, Shane's profile was active! And he had uploaded a photo from the time I had introduced him to my friend who worked for the Simpsons and we got an insider's tour of Film Roman Studios, the animation house where Bart and the gang come to life. And I was the photographer of the snapshot of him standing next to a life-size Homer Simpson. The photo displayed to attract potential love interests on this dating site.

D'oh!

I looked at the most recent login date shown on his profile and it was over Christmas! I had been watching his dog while he was with his family, looking for girls to date on the same site we had met almost a year earlier. I was furious! This was not at all how our story was supposed to conclude.

I was done with Shane. I was livid and ashamed and desperately disappointed.

Ross was right. The scales fell off of my eyes and I knew what a fool I had been for so many months. It was time to put an end to this non-relationship.

The next day was Martin Luther King Day and a school holiday. I stayed up late writing my indignant feelings in emancipation speech form. I didn't trust myself to wing it. There was truth Shane needed to hear and I had to stick to a script. It would take place over the phone as I had no intention of ever seeing him again. I was over him. Finally. Enough was enough.

Shane called me while I was driving out to see my parents and then on to the barn to ride DC. I feigned friendliness, accepted his call but told him I was in the middle of something and I would have to give him a call back in a few minutes. I knew I could not drive and preach simultaneously. I had not yet made it to the expressway so I pulled over on a residential street lined with post-war brick bungalows. I grabbed my neatly folded Word document out of my purse and nervously called Shane back.

He answered and launched into small talk. I shut that down by stating I had something I wanted to share with him. It got very quiet on his end. Calmly the words I had fit together into paragraphs the night before flowed out with an angry injustice. I didn't yell. I didn't cry. I just spoke the truth. And I could hear my heart beating in between each breath I took.

The truth was this was an unhealthy relationship. I had asked him to evaluate what we were to each other and why he hadn't stepped up. I felt betrayed he went behind my back, *while I was watching his dog*, and revived his online dating account to post photos I had taken of him in California. I had been upfront with him about my intentions and hopes for this friendship; why would he use me as a quasi-girlfriend while he was apparently in search of the real thing?!?!

There was a stunned silence on the other end of the line. When Shane finally began to talk, his voice quivered. He possibly was not prepared to hear these facts and receive the long-overdue ultimatum. I had pulled the rug out from under him as he had done to me repeatedly, although in a series of miniatures.

He said we could meet up to return the items he had of mine and vice versa. I said, "You can drop off my stuff on my porch and your stuff will be waiting for you. I don't want to see you." I said it and I really meant it. For the first time I was done with him.

Even though my words had been exacting and I did mean them wholeheartedly, I softened a bit and inserted a note into a book I had borrowed from him weeks before. I had self-respect and did not beg him to love me, but I told him things didn't have to be this way—he knew the proper way to create an alternate ending. I thought that might stir him up, enlivening his common sense.

He did not respond.

And it was okay.

I don't think it was an accident my emotional emancipation took place on Martin Luther King Day. Free at last. Free at last. Thank God Almighty.

ABOUT A YEAR after I broke up with the man who was never my boyfriend, Gail, the one I rode ponies with and who joined me for my nose revealing, visited me in Chicago, and we took Winnie to Montrose Harbor's Dog Beach. On our drive home in my Jeep Gail asked, "Whatever happened with that Shane guy?" I said I hadn't heard anything and I had no idea. I thought he was probably still around, still single.

"How could he be with someone if he's so unsure of life, not to mention selfish?" I wondered aloud. Within five minutes of Gail's remark, I did a double take as I saw a familiar looking guy with a familiar looking black dog in my peripheral vision. Shane was by himself, walking his dog on a deserted city sidewalk.

He looked a little sad.

CHAPTER 25

Middle Eastern Hospitality

IN THE WAKE of my breakup with Shane—if you could call it that since we weren't technically dating—an unwelcome yet unsurprising medley of relief, loneliness and despondency roosted on my heart. Riding DC was my therapy as my problems and heartache receded in the saddle.

DC's comfort was temporary—a slice of joy in the middle of gray. But since my new Illinois barn was 50 miles away, it was difficult to squeeze in rides during the workweek. Yet his soft nicker and heavy, sweet alfalfa breaths on my face momentarily relieved the twinge of my rejection.

Walking Winnie was sometimes healing and sometimes painful. Nothing can compare to the simple and pure love of a dog. My depleted heart and unrequited affections welcomed the salve of a doggie sneeze when I opened the door to my empty apartment. Her stubby metronome tail proved to me I was lovable and worthy, even if Shane couldn't see it. I had to alter our walking route somewhat so I wouldn't walk too close to his block and bump into him walking his dog. I avoided walking near the beach since that was where he lived.

Going to work was also a welcome break from the hurt because in the classroom my mind couldn't "go there." I steeled myself in order to deliver a solid English lesson and put on my best Ms. Friedland, professional educator. During the work day it was possible to shove my cast-off self, Susan the unwanted and undesirable, out of the way—at least until the students were dismissed at 4 p.m.

In the first few days following my Martin Luther King Day Independence Speech, I might have fooled my sixth graders, but I did not fool Ali, my colleague and friend who taught science. He was a sweet Turkish man with a pretty wife who had just had a baby. In the hallway after dismissal, he asked me how I was doing and I told him not good. I don't know why, but I shared my smarting loss with him. This was out of character for me—to tell someone I hadn't known that long, not to mention a male. But Ali's, "How are you?" was of the sincere "I care about you" variety—not the "I'm using this phrase as a polite greeting" style.

Ali responded immediately, "I could tell he was not the one for you."

His response startled me. How did Ali know? Shane had dropped by school one day and I had probably introduced him to Ali, but I don't think they interacted beyond a handshake and hello.

"He was not of your caliber. It was obvious." Ali in-

sisted my man was out there and proceeded to ask me
what I was doing that night.

"Nothing. Except for walking my dog."

"Well, I want you to come to my home and join my
wife and me as our special guest. My mother-in-law is still
in town and they have been preparing food all day. It will
be a wonderful feast."

I couldn't believe a man with a new baby was inviting
me, a workplace acquaintance, over for dinner. My
American friends fell off the map when they had new-
borns; they weren't entertaining guests or on the lookout
for the brokenhearted among them.

After walking Winnie under the dark January sky, I
drove several blocks to my co-worker's brick apartment
building. Ali opened the door wide, smiling and gave me a
pair of slippers to put on so I could leave my shoes at the
door. Immediately an elderly Turkish woman, his mother-
in-law, came to the entryway and said hello in Turkish
and brushed both my cheeks with her lips. Ali's brunette
wife smiled and said a quiet hello over the head of the
sleeping baby girl in her arms.

Ali showed me to the sofa and sat down next to me to
visit while the two women scurried around in the kitchen.
I felt like I should be helping them, and it felt odd I was
hanging out with a married man while his wife was
getting ready to serve us dinner. I shook it off, telling
myself to enjoy the hospitality and there were probably
cultural practices going on I couldn't quite understand.

Ali proudly showed me a beautifully decorated Koran
along with a black leather King James version Bible. He

was a devout Muslim, but wanted to also read the Bible. Next he produced his notebook of British idioms. Ali loved idioms. He used many American English idioms well. Some of them I had never heard of before, and it was especially apparent when he let me page through the notebook. We looked at one page together and I pointed out to him which ones I had never heard of.

"'Horses for courses,' I've never heard of that and I'm a horse lover. Have you used that before? I think you might need to figure out which ones work in America because I'm clueless on most of these." A knowing expression formed on Ali's face.

Dinner was served and we began with a soup.

"In Turkish cuisine, there is soup before every meal. We have hundreds of types of soups. It is very important for digestion. We even have soup for breakfast!" I don't know what the name of the soup was, but it was heavenly and warm. Just like the company.

In spite of the language barrier with his wife and his mother in law, the four of us carried on a lively conversation. The women were impressed with the fact I had a horse; that was apparently not common in Turkey. Ali mentioned he was going to be leading a school trip to Turkey in the summer and I should consider joining. He promised I would love it.

The older woman spoke Turkish to me and Ali translated, "She says you are beautiful and she really likes your hair."

Hi wife, who had been a dentist in Turkey before she and Ali moved to the States, softly offered, "You have very nice teeth. So straight and white."

I knew these women were on my side. I didn't ask, but I'm sure Ali had told them my sad Shane story. Even though I had never met the two before, they were perfectly executing the role of girlfriends.

After the multi-course meal ended in a fabulous cake-like dessert that took hours to make, we had Turkish coffee in the living room. The mother-in-law brought out a serving tray with medium sized porcelain cups holding what looked like a thick chocolate stew. It did not taste anything like chocolate. It was the most intense coffee I'd ever had in my life. I tried hard not to grimace, but the flavor had undertones of cigarette butts.

My fragile heart had found solace in the company of my Turkish friends for the evening. I received more cheek kisses upon my departure, and as I was about to step out back into the cold darkness, Ali said, "Thank you for coming, Susan. Now you have been here, you are family to us. Our home is your home. Please come back any time."

I still went home to a quiet and empty apartment, but my soul felt a bit more relaxed. I climbed the three flights of exterior stairs and opened the back door to my galley kitchen. I flipped on the light and the tap-tapping of dog toenails on hardwood coming from the living room signaled I was loved and in time, everything would be okay.

CHAPTER 26

Istanbul Taxi

SPRING IN THE Midwest equals resurrection. The land that lies gray, dead, and barren for six months finally decides to burst forth green, living, and fertile. The sun pauses in the sky a little longer each day, infusing hope into the regional psyche. Just when Midwesterners need it most, the occasional warm days of late April and early May signal to us the harshness is over and we know we will make it.

In the same way the shattered hope of a relationship-that-wasn't became easier to bear each day; however, I still fantasized Shane would come to his senses and reach out to me, saying he realized he couldn't live without me. Wasn't spring supposed to be an elixir that turned young men's hearts toward love?

Yet, in spite of the crocuses and budding leaves, I never heard from him—no emails, no texts, no phone calls, no notes at my door. Shane offered no apologies and had no apparent regret. Aside from the romantic feelings I had for him, it was undeniable we at least had possessed a strong friendship. How he could he have enjoyed the camaraderie and not have any remorse for hurting me so deeply? How did we go from friends in constant companionship to complete strangers living two blocks away from each other? Did he not feel the same intense loss I was experiencing?

Understandably, with the longer days and milder temperatures, my desire to ride increased to more than just on the weekend during daylight hours. I began escaping out to my barn sanctuary midweek after school. DC's shaggy, almost-black winter coat began to float off as I brushed him. If I had on fresh lip gloss, a gossamer veil of horse hair landed on my lips. Despite what the Ralph Lauren ads portray, being around horses is less glamor and more grime.

I began to occasionally take jumping lessons on DC. Even though he was 18, he moved well and could still jump a course like the show horse he was and always had been since I bought him a decade earlier. I was the one who needed the practice. Practice relaxing, practice being quiet in the saddle, and practice breathing. Funny how riding imitates real life.

Over the winter, in an effort to get out and meet people, I had picked up the sport of tennis. Once a week I went to an indoor club for lessons. It was not as fun as horseback riding, but in the depths of a Chicago deep freeze, it was yet another way to force myself out of my apartment and a way to be active. I publicized my latest hobby at work and at church in the hopes I could find friends to play with so I could improve my game and get out more.

One day in mid-May, a young science teacher down the hall invited me to play tennis with him and another colleague. Taner, the inviter, was a very sweet man, which I could tell from the few cordial conversations we'd had in the cavernous hallway of our brick school building. This was also evidenced in how he talked to the students when he looked them in the eye and listened to them intently.

I liked him—not *liked* him liked him, but I knew he was a good guy.

I knew prior to coming to Chicago he had been a principal of a school in Africa, but not much else. He had warm hazel eyes that smiled, not that I'd paid much attention. After all, he was a few inches shorter than me and a devout Muslim. I knew the tennis event wasn't a date because another teacher from work was going to be there too. This was safe.

The night of our tennis match, I showed up at the local park with my robin's egg blue Dunlop racquet and a can of new tennis balls. "You look like Steffi Graf!" Taner pronounced. I played with as much intensity as a beginning tennis player could muster. Hard-core tennis players would have cringed watching the three of us attempt to play, but at least we got a bit of exercise. We laughed, heckling ourselves and each other after ridiculous hits or swings and misses.

That tennis match led to a follow up trip to Starbucks with Taner, which led to going out for Chicago pizza—it was my duty. And that led to seeing movies together.

We weren't technically dating, since I would not consider dating someone with a different faith than mine. We were just enjoying each other's company, living in the moment and embracing a Chicago spring.

RIGHT AROUND THAT time Shane was no longer the first aching thought of my morning and the last aching thought of my evening. I anticipated a great summer because I had signed up to go to Turkey thanks to Ali's suggestions, and I was also going to buy a home in Chicago. I was going to be a full-blown adult.

Ross had business in Chicago and visited me in February, when I was newly in post-Shane emotional territory. He astutely observed, "Suz, you need to go somewhere that has already arrived, not stay in this "up and coming" neighborhood. It's not happening here." Once again, Ross had been right. First about Shane, and now on my choice of neighborhood. And so it was settled. I would move to "already arrived," mildly-upscale-without-being-pretentious Bucktown. Since I was planting my roots in Chicago, I would buy my own place there—with the help of my parents, of course.

AFTER A QUICK three trips out with my realtor, I discovered the ideal home: a three-level townhouse a block from the El. It had a garage, a granite and stainless kitchen, top-floor master suite with Jacuzzi jetted tub, in unit washer/dryer and a small patio. I signed the papers, and within a week I was a new homeowner and on a Turkish Air jet bound for Istanbul.

I didn't really know what to expect from the ancient city other than very tasty food; I had frequented a handful of local Turkish restaurants during the previous year thanks to the recommendations of my co-workers. There we had dined on flavorful kebab and stuffed grape leaves with a side of dill rice. The flavors popped.

Istanbul was more glorious than I would have ever imagined, rivaling Paris for the most beautiful international city. The dazzling former capital city of the Byzantine Empire, part Europe, part Asia had palaces galore and Roman ruins. The Grand Bazaar, which can trace its mercantile lineage back to the ancient Silk Road, and Emperor Justinian I's gorgeous church the Hagia Sophia with her majestic domes, were spectacular. But three things captivated my attention during the trip: Mado Ice Cream, the Turkish bath, and my Istanbul taxi ride on the last day.

Ali my math-colleague-turned-school-tour-guide delightedly introduced our group of a dozen travelers to Mado ice cream, a Turkish chain. After one trip to Mado, we quickly became obsessed. It was the creamiest of ice creams I'd ever had.

Like Pavlov's dogs, when our tour bus rounded a corner the students went crazy as they noticed the familiar all-caps blue letters of the Mado sign. "Mado! Can we get ice cream?" Ali, responsible guide that he was, said yes every time. After all, how often would our students be afforded such a pleasure?

Ali revealed to us toward the end of our trip the reason the ice cream had an inexplicably phenomenal taste was because it was made from goats' milk. And not just any goats. The Mado goats are from a certain region of Turkey where rich mountain grasses and the root of wild orchid were their dietary mainstay.

The second unforgettable aspect of Turkey was the hamam, otherwise known as the Turkish bath. After Istanbul we took a bus south to Antalya, the Turkish version of a Southern California beach town. There Audra, an eighth grader, her mom Pam and I saw a brochure image of smiling tourist lying flat on a hexagonal marble slab with a mound of pearly bubbles piled at least a foot high on his back. This was a Turkish bath, and the good news was our hotel had one. I wanted to get in on the pampering and unwinding.

Pam and I made appointments for the three of us for that afternoon. After arranging our times, we nervously pored over the Lonely Planet guide to hamams. The book said it was common for Turkish bathers to soak it all in sans clothing, but it also claimed it was okay to wear a swimsuit for the experience. It suggested simply wearing bikini bottoms. So that was my plan.

When the student, the mother, and I checked in at the hamam reception area, I was told there were only two female bath givers/attendants, but I could join my traveling companions if I was comfortable with a male. I stole a glance in the direction of the employees and noted both of the male attendants were in their 20s and were dark and handsome. I had never even had a massage back in the States from a male massage therapist. I didn't want to get too crazy in a foreign country. I declined, saying I would wait.

As mother and daughter disappeared into the hamam, the marbled room where the bathing took place, I was handed a towel with the dainty dimensions of a kitchen hand towel and told to wait. I undressed except for my black bikini bottoms and hoisted up the red checked towel over my torso. I tried to act nonchalant like I was used to walking around Turkish baths half naked and relaxing on cold, uncomfortable wooden chaise lounges, but there was no one around. I could only imagine what was going on inside the bath as shrill laughter periodically erupted.

The moment I heard Audra yell, "Bubbles!" I was supposed to enter the hammam and take a picture with her camera. When the signal sounded, I opened the door and my tour companions were lying flat on the marble slab, underneath mountains of bubbles looking up at me giggling, just like in the brochure. I took the lens cap off the camera and almost instantly the steam fogged the view.

When they were done I was next. I was in for a treat. What I didn't realize before I scheduled the Turkish bath is that it is a true bath: as in, your body gets washed. The caveat is someone else bathes you. In my case it was a Bulgarian woman who scrubbed and scrubbed me all over with some kind of a loofa sponge—in places I don't even scrub myself. To make matters worse, while she was presumably exfoliating every single pore on my body, the woman asked, "Do you have a husband?"

I shot back, "No. Do you?" while internally wincing, *"Why does everyone always ask that question? Around the world! Why are people so obsessed with whether you're married or not?"* Then I wondered if she could she tell from looking at my relatively naked body I was single and never married at 34? Was it so obvious I had been unlucky at love that even an Eastern European woman with little English could tell of my Western dating failures?

She responded, "Not anymore! My husband left me."

"Oh, I'm sorry."

She retorted, "I'm not!" and chuckled to herself.

Once I was all lathered up, she directed me to stand and said, "You are a big one," and then literally dumped a bucket of water over my head, dousing me from head to toe. The culminating humiliation was when she dried me all over with a huge fluffy white towel. I stood in front of her wearing nothing but my swimsuit bikini bottom, arms raised so she could wrap the towel around my back and buff my torso dry with back and forth motions.

When my glowing self was reunited with the mother daughter pair, Pam disclosed, "Part of the reason I was laughing so much was I was anticipating how you would respond. I know you're a lot more modest than I am, and I kept thinking, 'I can't picture Ms. Friedland having this done to her.'"

I felt mildly violated. In hindsight I was relieved there weren't three female bath givers, otherwise I would have been half-naked and in close proximity to a student and her mom. Mortifying.

After the harrowing hamam we stopped at an Internet café to check email. I wanted to let my parents know what I was doing and I was having a great time. I clicked on my Yahoo inbox and was floored to see an email from Shane titled "How to begin." I thought, "I wonder what this is all about," and began reading. My heart did not leap or skip a beat. Instead, I was skeptical.

Hello Susan.

This is something I've thought about a lot. How would I begin an email to you to say hello... I guess I would start it with "Hello Susan".(*Doesn't he know the period goes inside the quotation marks?!*)

I assume you're finished with teaching now. (*Of course I am, it's the beginning of July!!*)
I hope your year finished well.

I have wanted to write for a while to say hi and see how you were doing. But, of course, I also felt like I didn't want to presume that just because I feel like a lot of time has gone by and wanted to write doesn't mean you feel like getting an email from me. So, I won't make this long. But, I hope you're well. If this email isn't entirely unwelcome then maybe I'll hear from you sometime soon. If not, that's ok, too. But, I thought I'd knock on the door.

Shane

I was vindicated! This is what I had been waiting for all along! He missed me. He liked me, even if he couldn't admit it to himself—even if he wasn't man enough. He must have had some sliver of regret, hence the email.

For so many months I had been stymied, a shadow of my true self as I hung on, waiting for him to validate my desirability and womanhood by proclaiming us boyfriend and girlfriend. I was now so beyond him, and not just geographically speaking. The power had shifted since I had ended things, and he was the one to reach out to me first.

I relished this moment, and I couldn't pass up the opportunity to flaunt my awesome trip. After all, he had mentioned how he would love to go to Turkey one day. And so I responded just to rub it in a little, although it was difficult considering the Turkish keyboard was very different, as evidenced by my response.

I titled my email Merhaba which is the Turkish word for thank you. And I did not address him by name. That would have been too cozy. The guy had strung me along for months and months; I had no need for niceties. My well of graciousness had dried up months earlier.

I'm at an ýnternet cafe ýn Turkey now and was surprýsed by your message. I'm doýng well—thanks for askýng.

Thýs ýs an ýncredýble place! If you're ýnterested, I can gýve more detaýls on both myself and Turkey later.

And you?

Our group's last day in Istanbul was designated for shopping. I heard Taner was in Istanbul and he was going to come meet us. I was looking forward to seeing him. He possessed a special sparkle to his magnetic personality, and he was cute. His occasional lapse in proper English grammar was adorable. For example, he never used the word always, opting for the phrase "every time" instead. "When I speak to my mom in Turkey, she every time says, 'When are you coming back to Istanbul?'" or, "When Marco takes his science test, every time he gets an A."

Taner arrived at the Grand Bazaar, one of the world's first shopping malls, and of the two tour groups that were divided up to shop, he went with mine. We meandered through the maze of shops a few paces ahead of Audra and Pam.

Taner wanted to buy his sisters some jewelry and led me through a maze to a shop specializing in silver. "What do you like here?" he questioned.

I pointed to a turquoise and silver pendant on a silver chain. "This one's really cute." The shopkeeper agreed with me and gave it to Taner so he could help me try it on.

Taner nodded, then spoke to the shopkeepers in Turkish for a while as he was presumably wheeling and dealing to get jewelry for his female family members. I couldn't easily get the necklace off, so after a few attempts I gave up and decided to wait for Taner to help me remove it. He paid for his purchases, grabbed his shopping bag, and took my hand to leave.

"Wait! I'm still wearing the necklace. We forgot to give it back."

Taner smiled, "It's yours now." I protested and said I couldn't accept it. He rebutted saying it was a custom in Turkey for the locals to give gifts to visitors. I couldn't tell if this was true or if he was making that up so he could give me the necklace. It was confusing. And he kept holding my hand, which was also confusing. But it was extremely crowded in the mall and I looked very American. I thought he was holding my hand as a protective gesture.

Following the jewelry purchase we went to a rug store, where Taner chivalrously haggled in Turkish with the shopkeepers. I took it all in, impressed with the firmness yet friendliness of his negotiation. I didn't need to understand Turkish words to follow along in the discussion. About 20 minutes later after a lot of talking and some tea, the small kilim with warm red and dark blue geometric designs was mine.

I was somehow able to duck out from the school-sanctioned tour group and have dinner alone with Taner in the heart of the city. He chose an elegant, crowded restaurant with French café style seating along the Bosphorus Strait, an ancient sea route, the trading hub of the world during the fifth century. The palaces and elegant homes along the waterway were lit at night. It was magical.

During dinner I discovered the reason he was in the city was he had just been on a wife-hunting mission. No joke. He had made a trip to meet a woman who was a friend of a friend of a friend. He didn't care for her; she was rude. I was fascinated by this news. Someone I knew was actually in the process of arranging a marriage! Based on my lack of success, this sounded like an appealing option.

We drew glances from onlookers. Was it the height difference or the way we looked together—tall strawberry Capri-wearing woman with a shorter, obviously Turkish man at her side?

For dessert, Taner took me to Mado in a swanky neighborhood; the streets were packed with people around 11 at night. The Istanbul night scene made Chicago seem like a sleepy rural village. A potpourri of cultures coursed through the streets. From women in black burqas with only their eyes exposed, to women who wore bright colors yet their heads were covered to conceal their hair, to others in completely Western dress, to women dressed very scantily. The parade of colors was mesmerizing.

After dessert, Taner hailed a taxi and escorted me back to the hotel. The hand holding continued in the cab, and I basked in the sweetness of the gesture. Maybe we both had a little crush on each other. It was all very innocent—he was searching for a Turkish bride and I didn't take him seriously since we were culturally and religiously worlds apart. I could not envision myself wearing a veil and praying toward Mecca five times a day, but he was my friend and because of him I'd had an amazing day. After months of a relational void, it was fun to have butterflies a-fluttering in my stomach and to dine and laugh with someone again.

I was ending my Turkish trip on a high note. While these thoughts swirled through my brain, I was surprised when Taner suddenly leaned in and kissed me on the lips just as the taxi rolled past the towering stone arches of the Roman Aqueduct.

I laughed aloud and then had to explain I wasn't the kind of person who would kiss a co-worker. I hadn't been kissed in longer than I could remember. Being in an exotic foreign country was just too much!

We made awkward small talk for the remainder of the taxi trip. He walked me up to my hotel room. I thought he was going to just see me at the door and say goodbye, but instead he walked right in, sat on the bed for a second and commented, "This is a nice room."

I was uncomfortable that he was so comfortable in my room. Ali was a few doors down, and even though he was younger than me by a few years, I felt him take on a fatherly protection of me during this trip. Students were in nearby rooms too, and I didn't want to give off the wrong impression about Mr. Taner and Ms. Friedland. I think Taner sensed my skittishness regarding the situation so he gave me a hug and left.

I literally did not know if I would ever see him again because he wasn't sure if his visa would be extended so he could teach another year at our school. It didn't matter, because it wasn't like we could have a future together. Yet it did matter, because my heart was blooming.

Regardless of his wife search and our opposing worldviews, I had developed a warm affection for the adorable science teacher down the hall.

CHAPTER 27

Bucktown and the Buckaroo

BUCKTOWN IS A Chicago neighborhood located near the bustling six-corner intersection of Milwaukee, North, and Damen Avenues where hipsters, young families and senior citizens saunter and shuffle along the awkward intersection that is the heart of the community. Diverse architectural styles ranging from turn of the century to sleek and modern, to sleek and modern designed to look turn of the century line the residential streets. There is a small gourmet grocery store, red brick library, at least three dog parks nearby and a walk-up Starbucks where you can order your latte from the sidewalk through a window. Part of the charm is the intermittent roar of the El as it passes by. It was fairly safe for a single girl and home to dozens of shops; I was thrilled to be its newest resident.

I moved into my townhome soon after my return from Turkey. The first afternoon I took Winnie for a walk down the block of my new neighborhood, a young dad and his toddler were playing in the front yard of their red brick row house from the 1800s.

The father gawked as I passed. "We have one of those. Wait here." He jogged up the front steps as I paused on the sidewalk puzzled; a split second later, out trotted a red female Doberman that could have been Winnie's sister, except for the random flecks of white hair.

It was a good sign.

I began to set up house, painting my townhouse in a color palette of mocha tones for the main living areas and spa green for my master bathroom. I even had new window treatments installed to block my neighbors across the alley from peering into my living and dining area. Not to say they were peeping Toms, but it was close quarters in that urban world, kind of like the movie *Rear Window*.

Even though I was single and would rather not be, I felt satisfied I now had a nice home in a nice neighborhood with a wonderful dog and an amazing horse. But my longing for my own family like the sweet dad, Doberman, and baby chided my daily. I was living 3/4 of the American Dream.

Beth, a friend who is as close as a little sister, began going to pastry school, and since my place was a convenient walk to the El, she moved in. I was no longer alone.

As I walked Winnie down the city streets three times a day—before breakfast, after work, and before bedtime—I had plenty of time to muse. A recurring thought flirted for my attention: maybe I would have to move to a foreign country to find a husband. Apparently girls like me were a dime a dozen in the States.

If I traveled to Argentina or even Ireland (I'd had such

a wonderful adventure there on my riding vacation), my strawberry blonde hair, height, or American accent might make me stand out in the crowd. Instead of blending in, I imagined I could be exotic or at least charming to someone in a foreign country. Maybe I'd have a chance at love elsewhere! Just as I swooned when I heard a French accent, perhaps my Chicaaago accent would be endearing to someone from overseas. It had already done the trick on a man from the Middle East. Now couldn't I deploy my "skill" elsewhere?

When I had moved back to Illinois, I started attending a church with services welcoming to people of any racial or ethnic background—a place where people of all phases of their spiritual journey could come together to explore questions of faith. The worship leader's wife was African by way of Sweden. My Bible study leader was of mixed ancestry and from South Africa. There were families from various South American countries. Keeping that in mind, I didn't count on being viewed as exotic and thereby on the radar of a foreigner within my church, foreign by way of Canada.

Quinn was from a small town in Canada and a self-proclaimed horse whisperer. He was also one of the attendees of a Bible study I joined.

Quinn had worked for one of the carriage companies that pull tourists in a Cinderella-type coach around Water Tower Place. I think he might have even worked for Medieval Times. That was interesting. However, as I got to know him, I found out several things about his character making me question his sanity:

1. He was lactose intolerant and used it against people he didn't like. Namely a boss. He told a story of how he and his boss had to take a long trip to a job in the dead of winter. Quinn was mad at the boss and so he intentionally ordered a milkshake from McDonald's prior to hitting the road. He knew this would make him gassy and so he shared with our group how he basically passed gas the whole two hours in the car with his boss, smirking all the while.

2. He wound up in jail for supposedly intervening when he saw a boyfriend and girlfriend duking it out on the streets. This fact came about one week when our group leader asked everyone, "So how's your week going so far?" Quinn responded, "Well, it would be better if I hadn't wound up in the clinker." Suddenly the handful of troublesome students I was dealing with seemed like a mundane issue.

3. He once worked at a small airport as a squirrel sharpshooter. Or maybe it was mouse. A Canadian airport in the middle of nowhere had been plagued by rodents, making landing dangerous. So it was his job to kill them, thus saving air travelers from the perils of vermin on the runway. At least that's what he told us.

Quinn found out I had a horse and used that piece of info as his entrée. Normally when one horse lover meets another horse lover, there's a strong connection point. This typically starts with, "What kind of riding do you do? Do you have your own horse? What breed?" In the case of finding out we had a mutual interest, I kept the details of DC on the DL. Just because we were both single horse lovers, it didn't mean we were meant to be together. Even if we lived in the same city and went to the same church.

Once I moved into my townhouse, I suggested to our small group we could have some of the meetings at my place. I wanted to have people over, as I was still trying to make new friends. Besides having a dog to come home to, nothing makes a house feel more like a home than having it frequented by friends. And so they came.

At the conclusion of one group meeting, Quinn commented that my overhead light in my family room was quite bright, and offered to install a dimmer switch for me. I sensed where this proposition was headed, but I liked the idea of having dim lights, so I said sure.

Quinn insisted on buying the dimmer materials himself, and said he would arrive early to group the next week. I felt kind of uncomfortable around him, although I couldn't quite pinpoint the reason. Thankfully Beth was going to be home too at the time of his early arrival.

Quinn showed up at my door wearing a tool belt, clutching a plastic Home Depot bag. I led him up my stairway to the family room, where he then put on a headlamp before installing the dimmer switch. It was both awkward and enlightening.

About a week after the dimmer switch episode, Quinn called me while I was driving home from the barn.

"I'd like to train your horse. I'm kind of like Monty Roberts, the horse whisperer." I did not laugh aloud at this preposterous comparison. Instead I was mildly incensed. Comparing oneself to the likes of Monty Roberts is along the line of a community theater actress comparing herself to Meryl Streep. His words were audacious.

"That's nice of you to offer, but my horse is already pretty well trained. I've had him for years; he's a show horse. We already get along well. Not to mention, I take riding lessons with a trainer at my barn."

Quinn was not going down without a fight. He started to explain he had horse training methods good even for horses already trained. I shut him down with my refusal, comforting myself, *You don't want to entrust someone with your horse that you don't like having around your dog.*

A few weeks earlier I'd glimpsed him trying to pet Winnie with his foot when I had already warned my small group guests Winnie was afraid of feet. She looked up at him with a sliver of white in her eye showing and shot out of the way from his intimidating foot. I said, "She's afraid of feet. Don't touch her like that!" and he smiled a smug, creepy smile in response to my admonition.

WHILE I WAS trying to be active in my church community in the hopes of meeting new friends of both sexes and possibly even someone to date, my whirlwind Istanbul romance, if you could call it that, was kind of on again.

A few weeks into the new school year I began walking

a delicate tightrope between friendship and something more with my Turkish co-worker. I viewed our evening on the town in Istanbul two months earlier (and the taxi kiss) as an impulsive aberration to our friendship. However, that was just the starting point for what turned out to be a dating relationship, without the label of a dating relationship. After all, he had spent his summer meeting women for a potential arranged marriage, and I was still active on a couple of Internet dating sites. We both had a relational goal in mind. He journeyed down the path of the ancients, and I was futuristic as an early adopter of Internet dating.

One day during this era Beth announced as she came home from work, "You won't believe who I saw when I got off the train this morning! Ryan Rollins!"

"No way! Did you talk to him? Did he see you? What was he doing? How did he look?"

She gave me the pertinent details: yes he was still cute, and it looked like he was going to work. We had heard through the grapevine he was an attorney. Maybe he was on his way to court. How sexy. Now why hadn't I lightened up and gone on that date with him in high school? The one where he broke my heart by calling to say he had intended on inviting me to the Valentine's Day banquet but had "something suddenly come up." Maybe I wouldn't currently be in my online dating, quasi-dating a Muslim, Quinn-dodging dilemma.

Since I seemed to be a magnet for the wrong guys, I decided to hunker down in my townhouse with my dog and my roommate and despite the hour-long commute, go to the barn where life made sense—around the horses.

I tried to reassure myself I didn't need a man—I had something even better—a horse. DC was, in fact, still my dream come true. None of my other single friends had such a dapper supporting actor in their lives. And none of my married friends did either. Occasionally I dabbled in what one girlfriend called "video games for girls"—the online dating world, but not with much success.

My love life was a bleak Chicago winter. Some days there were glimpses of sunshine, but mostly they dragged on bitterly cold and deeply gray.

CHAPTER 28

The Unraveling

TANER AND I started out the school year cordially in spite of our brief romantic interlude. I felt awkward knowing we had a one-day romance in Istanbul, but was confident the clarification email I shot off afterward I realized our whirlwind day in Istanbul was meant to be an isolated incident and not the start of a long-time romance, and his understanding response was the end of that chapter. I told him it was an isolated incident and not the start of a romance. We could move forward on a friendly, yet professional level and that aberration—the taxi kiss—would have no bearing on the new school year.

However, as much as I did not want to admit it to myself or anyone else, seeing him at work was the highlight of my day, every day. He looked quite handsome in his crisp dress shirt adorned with a classic tie. His wide smile and sparkling hazel eyes greeted me every morning. That didn't exactly help things. Nor did his ongoing kindness. He was the most gentlemanly man I had ever encountered, holding doors open, asking, "How are you?" and really meaning it, and finding little ways to make my life easier.

I was a practical girl. I knew marrying a Muslim would not work out in the long run, although the church guys I had been interested in were not interested in me. Quinn, the self-proclaimed horse whisperer, didn't count. So, in spite of my better judgment, Taner and I evolved into somewhat of an item—serious, but not too serious.

If that is even possible.

The official start to our unofficial relationship began the hot August afternoon we went to the beach after school. Lake Michigan was only a few blocks away from work. We sat on the pier for a while talking. He told stories of his family and of his time teaching in Africa. We jumped into the water and before I knew it, he scooped me up and twirled me around, my feet dangling in the brisk water, tracing a circle. This was not something two colleagues would do together. This was a boy-friend/girlfriend activity. It felt like we were in a Nicholas Sparks novel.

Following the beach, we began to see each other regularly. We'd go to a movie or to coffee or out to dinner. He would hold my hand and always pay for me. I even took him swing dancing once. It wasn't really his cup of tea. But actual tea was. So we'd go out for tea.

I knew I had a secret relationship. Secret because it would look bad from a professional level, and secret because I did not want to break my mother's heart. Secret because I knew our versions of God would not match up in the long run.

In the back of my mind, I knew I was slowly breaking my own heart with every dinner out, movie, discussion of religion, pleading for me to move to Turkey and my "no" response.

I was not in a good place.

Meanwhile, my friend Amy who was working in a remote village in India found the love of her life on eHarmony (even though he was in Korea). I was asked to be a bridesmaid in her wedding in Malibu in January. If it worked for her, maybe someday, it could work for me too.

My 35th birthday party rolled around in October, and Ross flew into town and sent out an Evite for the 20th anniversary of my teenage birthday. Chef Beth made the cupcakes. A handful of people showed up, but Taner was not among them. He was invited. I understood it would have been strange to have him there. And how would I introduce my secret Muslim boyfriend to my church friends? That alone was proof our fling could not materialize into a full-fledged dating relationship.

Christmas arrived and Beth and I hosted another party. The guest list was long but Quinn, the supposed horse whisperer, was not on it. I felt bad, but he made me so uncomfortable and I wanted to enjoy the evening. Taner did not come, as he had flown back to Turkey for the long holiday break. There was musical entertainment in the form of a saz, a Middle Eastern stringed instrument like a lute, that my friend/coworker Ali played. That was the first and probably the last time I'll hear a saz at a Christmas party.

It was almost a year from ending my relationship-that-wasn't with Shane. He was such a thing of the past. Taner was not. He came to visit me as soon as he returned to Chicago from his trip back home.

Swept up in the moment, he kissed me with gusto. Less than a minute passed, and he burst out. "I can't do this! I'm a very bad man," and began to weep, tears rolling down his cheeks as he explained, "The reason I didn't contact you over winter break is I got engaged. But I don't love her. I love you. Why won't you marry with me?"

His small grammar mistakes like "marry with me" were endearing.

This revelation simultaneously surprised and did not surprise me. He had hinted before I should go with him to Turkey. His family owned a hazelnut orchard near the sea shore. He said we could have a little house there and I could teach English. The idea of such a romantic existence made my heart beat faster, but again, the practical Midwestern girl in me would not let my heart go crazy. I was Emma Thompson's character in *Sense and Sensibility*—just too sensible.

"You know I can't. Long-term we would kill each other. We disagree on too much and over time that would just get bigger."

"In Africa there are Christians married to Muslims and Muslims married to Christians. It's okay."

I reminded him as lovely as that sounded, we would end up breaking each other's hearts. "You need a nice Turkish girl. We can't do this anymore. It just hurts too much. And it's not right."

He left my townhouse for the last time, but not before we embraced in a clutching grasp. We exchanged a feather of a kiss on the lips and said goodbye in a classic, old movie fashion.

But it was not really goodbye since our classrooms were across the hall from each other.

My heart hurt. But at the same time, a wave of relief washed over me. I had just loved and lost someone who was not meant to be my lifelong love.

The sting of emptiness was my new companion, but at least I knew one thing: I was lovable *and* I knew how to give love. I held my head high. This provided confirmation I *was* good at loving someone! I had what it took to be in a relationship—with a man—and it wasn't my fault nothing had come together for me in that category. It just wasn't the right timing.

My soul felt most at peace when I could retreat to the barn, get in the saddle, and view my world through the perked brown ears of DC. In those moments I was granted reprieve from the heaviness of my loneliness.

And the affection percolating in my heart, devotion I longed to lavish upon a husband perfect for me, was not wasted but showered upon my tall, dark, and handsome bay partner for the last 10 years.

My adoration had a worthy recipient.

CHAPTER 29

California Scheming

FOR A SINGLE person wanting to be married, there is nothing as uncomfortable as going to a wedding alone where all the other guests will be married, except for babies, little kids, and teens. It's like salt in a wound. The only way around the "I'm not married and I'm here alone" awkwardness is to be part of the wedding party so you have an exact role, a function.

Instead of feeling like a loser, I prepared to hold my head high knowing I was like a back-up dancer. My very presence would add to the overall beauty and enjoyment of the audience. I was bringing the extra pizazz. At least that's what I kept telling myself as I boarded a plane bound for L.A. to be in the bridal party of my friend Amy.

This occurred only a few weeks after the revelation my colleague/love interest was *for real* engaged. I had not returned to California since I moved back to Chicago a year and half earlier. The dead of winter was the perfect time to head back for a Golden State wedding and catch up with a few of my friends in Los Angeles.

My former roommate Heidi had a spare bedroom in what had been "our" apartment for several years, the 1920s butter-yellow house with the pink camellia tree by the front door. I planned to stay with her the first night of my California return. It just so happened she was having a birthday party for our friend Sabrina. When I set foot in my old digs, several friends from my California life were celebrating. The party-goers' laughter and candles glowing on the balcony greeted me.

I walked up the stairs from which I had ripped off the old mud-brown carpet and painted over it a fresh purpley brown about six years earlier. I thought about how audacious it was Heidi and I hadn't told the landlord, rationalizing the carpet was at least 30 years old and harboring terrible germs. We were actually doing him a favor by way of free home improvement.

When I stepped into the living room, I caused quite a stir. I felt a little shy with the attention zeroing in on me all at once. Many of my friends from our 30-somethings church group paused their conversations to encircle me in their embraces. The aspiring actress, the animator, the entrepreneur, the ad-man were all there, unchanged, and that comforted me.

"Susan! How ARE you?"

"Sooo good to see you? How's life in Chicago?"

"Hi, friend!"

It was nice to know my friends hadn't forgotten me.

The party was a blur as I shared the Cliff's Notes version of the last year and a half I'd been away. I left out the painful parts about Shane leading me on and having fallen for someone whom I could never marry because he was Muslim and engaged. I was honest, but not entirely open. I reserved that for Heidi, who was like a sister to me after having been my roommate for almost a decade.

I slid under the bedspread mid-party with earplugs nestled in my ears. The two hour time difference between L.A. and Chicago was not in my favor, and I had a big day in store with a return visit to my school followed by a drive to Malibu and connecting with Amy and her wedding party.

The bed was not as comfortable as my new pillow-top mattress in Bucktown. The bathroom was dated and kind of dumpy with an ever-present damp smell. The balcony sagged. My newish brick townhouse in Chicago was so much nicer than this ancient rental, yet I slept well in my old home, even with the background droning of party voices.

THE NEXT MORNING the California sun shone and flowers bloomed everywhere. There is a reason Pasadena's Tournament of Roses Parade happens every year on January 1. The story goes Midwesterners who had escaped the brutal winters by settling in Los Angeles decided to plan an event to arouse interest and a little envy from their families and friends "back East."

I had just journeyed from a land of dirty snow, windshields needing scraping, and where breathing out of your mouth was an observable event. The night before, I had stepped out of LAX and into the night air and I didn't freeze!

The 60-70 degree temperatures of SoCal and roses in bloom made me feel 10 years younger, and something began stirring inside.

I returned to the middle school where years earlier I had discovered my calling in life was to be a teacher. I wanted to drop by and say hello. Students buzzed in the middle of the quad during their lunch break. A cluster of them squealed my name and clamored to give me hugs near the ancient anchor that was the focal point of the school yard.

One eighth grade boy I had as a sixth grader approached me with hands on hips scolding, "Where have you been?" He was the one who had sent me a love letter two years earlier, complete with a picture of the two of us together with hearts floating above our heads. Nevermind we were both stick figures and my lines were twice the height of his. That simple gesture made me smile, and assured me if an 11-year-old could see my value and express affection for me, somewhere an older version might just happen along my path.

After seeing the kids, I popped into the staff lounge where I knew the majority of the teachers, my colleagues for five years, would be gathered eating their lunches.

"Hi Susan!" the homemaking teacher smiled. "Wait! Susan? What are you doing here? It seemed so natural to see you in this room it didn't hit me at first—you're back!" And so began the warm reunion with my work friends. I repeated a shorter version of the spiel I had given to my friends at the birthday party the night before when they asked, "How's Chicago?"

Driving the rental car away from Arcadia, I reflected on how happy the students were to see me and how welcoming my old coworkers had been. The San Gabriel mountains rising against the backdrop of the San Gabriel Valley looked taller and more majestic than I remembered them. The weather was perfect; I didn't even have to wear a coat.

In the middle of January.

My heart was full at the end of my short visit as I moved on to the wedding in Malibu and bade farewell to the mountains, my school, my home.

I HADN'T SEEN my swing dance buddy Amy in a couple of years. Around the same time I moved to Chicago, she left as a missionary to India. The last time we were together, she was preparing to leave for service. Amy was an occupational therapist and had signed on for two years to literally change the lives of disabled children in remote villages. She packed medical supplies and made arrangements to have wheelchairs from the United States delivered to her village in India. In short, she was a younger, Protestant version of Mother Theresa.

I helped her prepare for her overseas adventure by

removing the inner cardboard from multiple rolls of toilet paper so she could pack her bags more efficiently. Apparently using toilet paper was not the norm for the rural area where she was headed. She told me she didn't even want to think about what she'd do if her supply of TP ran out.

About a year into Amy's stay in the middle of India, she met her man on eHarmony. Although from the United States, he was in South Korea at the time. After several lengthy phone calls, he invited her to visit.

I parked the rental car and prayed for confidence as I would not know any of the bridal party and guests. I was not only the sole single bridesmaid, I was the only non-Californian. This weekend was going to stretch me outside of my comfort zone.

"Amy!" I tightly embraced my sweet brunette friend when I met her in the hotel lobby. She was beautiful before, but now had that extra special bride glow. Her hair was shiny and much longer than I remembered, and she had lost weight.

"You're so thin!"

"It's amazing when you have nothing to do in a foreign country but ride an exercise bike while watching episodes of *Little House on the Prairie* every night!"

We caught up in our hotel room and then I met the mysterious groom I had heard so much about as we were heading out to the rehearsal dinner. He had grown up as a missionary kid in a small village in Mexico. I knew my friend had met her match, one with mettle and shared values.

The site of the wedding had once been a ranch, and the ceremony was going to be outside on the lawn adjacent to a rustic lodge. Oak and eucalyptus trees lined the location, and a delicate waterfall bubbled along the flagstone pathway that led to the seating.

Guests began arriving while the bride and our bridal party preened, perfecting our hair and makeup. The wedding coordinator ushered us to the just-out-of-the-way spot on the patio where we lined up for the procession. I glimpsed the overall view of the venue, supportive friends and family seated, guitarist strumming, flowers and tulle adorning the aisle and arbor area. I was happy for Amy although the fleeting, yet recurring question "Will this ever happen for me?" flickered in my mind. The nagging thought was interrupted by the coordinator. "We're ready for you!"

Crack!

Gasp.

Crash!

"Oh no!"

Nervous giggles shot out from most of the bridesmaids.

Instead of carrying traditional bouquets, we were supposed to carry small wrought iron lanterns with a spray of flowers wrapped on the top. For unknown reasons, as we picked up our lanterns, which we had set down as we waited for our perfect timing to walk down the aisle, they fell apart. Glass spewed across the path where the bride would soon be walking.

Only one bridesmaid had a still-intact lantern.

The wedding coordinator made the quick decision for us to unwind the wire attaching the corsage size cluster of flowers on the lantern, and carry them as our bouquets. We left the shards of glass behind and began our aisle journey sporting the miniature bouquets. Hopefully the guests would be so enthralled with our black, fur-rimmed sweaters atop our burgundy A-lined skirts and bridal party smiles, no one would notice our teensy floral arrangements.

Despite the flower fiasco, the rest of the ceremony proceeded in textbook fashion. The bride and groom gazed adoringly into each other's eyes and then sauntered down the aisle as husband and wife.

If Amy could meet her husband while in a remote village in India, I could certainly meet one living in a major city of the United States.

Even as an introvert.

Even though I seemed to attract the self-proclaimed horse whisperers of the world.

Even if the winters were brutal and no one in the city wanted to go outside to be social.

The wedding that started out with the potential to be painfully awkward and mock my 30-something singleness instead served to fan a flicker of hope.

And, as much as I hated to admit it, it took me leaving California and then coming back again for a visit to realize it had indeed become my home.

PART VI

Calm and Forward

CHAPTER 30

Grooming for a Takeover

"Is that DC?" asked a young woman striding past me on a large chestnut in the warm up ring at the Midwest's horse show mecca, Lamplight Equestrian Center. It was early June, a time traditionally known for weddings, and I was at a horse show.

DC trotted on the lunge line, rhythmically placing hooves forward in diagonal pairs in the taupe footing, creating a large circle of which I was the center. I willed him to unleash his Thoroughbred energy before I mounted.

"Yes it is. I remember you," the face looked familiar, although I was acquainted with the teenage version of the young woman from attending horse shows for one season together 12 years prior.

From the saddle she reintroduced herself to me. "I thought I recognized that face. He has that distinctive blaze. He looks great! How old is he now?"

I thanked her, told her he was old enough to vote, filled her in on our move from Illinois to California and then back home to Illinois, and inquired about her riding history since I'd seen her last.

I explained it was our first show in a really, really long time and I was there to have fun. "I live and teach in the city now and am kind of a weekend rider. I'm not here for ribbons." We were a comfortable team, but technically a longshot.

When I was with DC in the sanctuary of the country stable, I was not the single girl who couldn't find a good guy, the one about whom people wondered, "She's so sweet and pretty, so why isn't she married by now?" I was not an old maid. I was a horsewoman.

When I was at the horseshow, I was an *equestrian*. I participated in the same passion as the Queen of England and Jackie Kennedy. I felt regal even if I didn't get to accept the trophy and insert a blue ribbon into the browband of DC's fancy-stitched bridle.

My equestrian identity possessed an air of nobility and accomplishment. The 30-something women of my Chicago neighborhood clad in skinny jeans walking their dogs hand in hand with their husbands or boyfriends had nothing on me. I walked in my Tailored Sportsman breeches not with a husband, but a magnificent 1,200 pound Kentucky-bred Thoroughbred with a swift river of a stride.

I didn't need the knight, I had the horse.

After about 10 minutes of trotting, five minutes in each direction, I reeled DC in, unsnapped the lunge line and led him to the mounting block. I thought of how happy I was to be home and brushed away our uncertain future by living in the moment.

"SUSAN, IF YOU want to come back, you can have my teaching position. I'll leave all my files. You can have everything." Mary, my friend and former co-worker, revealed a secret when I had dropped by my former school en route to Amy's wedding in January. She was going to retire in a few months.

An elementary school teacher for years until she switched to middle school, Mary possessed perfect penmanship and an immaculate classroom with bright bulletin boards displaying excellent student work. She exuded organization and motherly warmth.

During my whirlwind first year of teaching, Mary unconsciously mentored me as we formed a friendship. I would always be indebted to her for her generosity, and this offer was tempting.

I had only been in my new Chicago townhouse for seven months and it seemed rather irresponsible to move halfway across the country and start a new life.

Besides, I was Midwestern through and through. I belonged to the flat land of green cornfields and silvery skyscrapers. I had learned how to use the El and was enjoying Chicago's Dog Beach and the countryside's wide open pastured horse farms. How could I leave behind my family, my new home, my barn, and DC?

Yet as much as I loved my family and the Midwest for what it offered DC, I was weary of big city life. My social circle was shrinking, not expanding. I hadn't had any success in the dating realm. In California I felt like the single yet somewhat popular girl. In Illinois I was the unmarried schoolmarm when I wasn't with DC, which was most of my day-to-day existence.

I didn't want to move DC again. It didn't seem fair to him. The multi-day trailer ride from California to Illinois had taken a toll. He had lost weight and the area above his eyes had an unfamiliar sunken in look when we reunited back home. Mary's job offer was simultaneously exciting and disturbing.

I WALKED DC on a loose-ish rein over to the ring where the hunter course was set up. This was the same show-grounds where I took him 12 years earlier.

As the horse and rider in the arena cantered through their course, I made mental notes trying to remember the simple yet complex pattern. I was fully present, my mind fixed on trying to remember the correct order of the eight two-and-a-half-foot fences.

Riding a horse is the practice of being in the moment. In fact, when you're around a horse, there is no time to worry about external problems looming insurmountably. Horses give their humans a mini-vacation, a respite from life's troubles. Their mere presence opens a portal to a realm where stress and sadness do not exist. In the saddle I didn't worry about whether or not I'd ever meet a man who reciprocated affection and desire for me. It didn't matter from 16.3 hands high. The decision I had made months earlier was far from consideration.

"You know your course?" my trainer asked. I nodded and then pointed my finger and drew the outside line, angle, angle, outside line course pattern.

THE TINY VILLAGE of Wayne, Illinois—Horse Heaven on earth—felt like a place I belonged. It was home without my ever having lived there.

My history inhabited the showgrounds and adjoining fields. Across the street from the horse show was the backyard farm where I first learned to ride on Jim Dandy and other borrowed horses. The cemetery where we horse crazy girls jumped over headstones was across the street too. A few miles down the road was the giant red barn from the 1800s, the site of the fox hunt where I had ridden Jim Dandy once as a guest. In the forest preserve across Dunham Road I jump judged for an advanced three-day event circa 1983, and saw future Olympic equestrian Torrance Watkins-Fleischmann. She smiled and acknowledged me as we passed each other on foot.

Most of my memories attached to this prairie land of small neighborhoods with backyard stables ushered in joy. Yet the pristine showgrounds lined with crabapple trees that bloomed, showing off their lacy branches every April was also the scene of one indelible experience my brain could replay flawlessly even though it happened 20 years before.

It was a summer day and I was wearing my too-big Harry Hall breeches bought from my older sister's friend who had sold her horse. The horse girl posse I rode with almost daily that summer had walked the horses across the street to take group lessons. "My mom and dad said I could join Pony Club," I smiled at the local three-day event trainer who was an A Pony Club graduate.

Standing near Jim Dandy's bright red withers, she turned her face to me. "If you join, you'd need to have new boots." Mine were tall rubber boots. "And a new saddle." My saddle wasn't really *my* saddle. It was Cindy's. "And you need to have your own horse."

That was a lie! I had read a Pony Club brochure the lady at the second-hand tack shop had given me from cover to cover. It clearly stated to get started, all you needed was *access* to a horse. Jim Dandy was not *my* horse, but I rode him more than his owner.

Next, the trainer looked to my friend riding a large bay pony. "*You* should really join Pony Club." When the girl said the horse wasn't hers but technically her grandmother's the trainer said, "Let's meet with your grandmother and wine her and dine her and speak to her about how Pony Club would be perfect for you. You've got a talented pony here."

I was too timid to say anything to counter the trainer's false claim. Instead, I carried the hurt deep within me, my little secret. My friend and her grandmother's pony were good enough. I was not.

As an adult, lunging a horse and getting ready to show

without the assistance of my trainer meant I was good enough. Here I was with my own beautiful horse about to enter the competition. I had a right to be on this turf where the local eventing celebrity trainer told the 12-year-old me I wasn't good enough.

I found out later the same trainer who smashed my girlhood dream had been working toward competing in the Olympics. She never made it. Apparently she wasn't good enough.

WEARING MY NEW a navy hunt coat, butter yellow ratcatcher and Ariat field boots, I entered the arena and picked up a trot along the rail, then circled to the right as the competitor who had jumped the course before me walked out the gate. I sat a couple of beats and then used my outside leg to press onto DC's side and held the right rein steady. He cantered and I finished the circle and then set off toward the first jump.

DC loved jumping and knew his job. My goal was to breathe and pilot him to the correct fences, interfering as little as possible with his movement. I began to count, "One, two, one, two, one, two."

He made it to the first fence and sailed right over it. It was a straight shot to the second fence so I squeezed my reins like sponges ever so slightly to regulate his pace.

One, two, three, four, five, six, jump! We got the proper number of canter strides down the first line and I turned my head slightly to look for the next line.

DC'S TRANSITION BACK to the Midwest was not as easy as I had thought it would be. He lost a shoe almost immediately upon arriving, and the farrier was not able to come out for a week. The proprietor of the Andalusian farm where I short-term boarded him until a stall was available closer to my home told me her husband could pull the other shoes so he would at least be barefoot all the way around until the farrier arrived. Bad idea.

The next time I saw him, he walked like a person accustomed to wearing shoes traversing a rocky beach. And because he was not able to be ridden and was delighted in his new pasture freedom, he was a wild man.

My two sisters went with me to see my old/new horse, and when we led him from the stall to the pasture, a brown tornado swirled back and forth, snorting with his tail held high, Arabian style. He was scary. Renee said, "I'm going to tell mom!"

Thankfully a stall opened at the 100-acre horse farm, Tower Hill. There I would have trainers and regular access to a farrier. This beautiful facility with the largest indoor arena I had ever seen, is where DC and I would grow old together—until the plan changed.

I LOOKED FOR the center of the third fence and positioned my hands and legs evenly, forming a chute for DC to travel through. My bay boy felt like he was speeding toward the in gate. Horses know which direction home or their temporary stall is.

His thundering stride matched the unfolding of my life's plan: both felt a little out of control and potentially unsafe. DC cantered faster than he should have and left out a stride between fences. I knew he was going too fast down the line, yet I tried to portray a demeanor of control. I spoke quietly to him saying whoa and easy. He needed reassurances and so did I.

"I'M 90 PERCENT sure I'll say yes, but can I think about it and get back to you tomorrow?"

I sat at my black desk in the mustard entryway of my Bucktown condo. I had just spoken to my former middle school principal. He had extended a job offer for Mary's position. I had to move back to California. It was going to break my heart. I would not only have to say goodbye to my parents and my sister and her family, but also to DC.

I couldn't bear the thought of dragging my beloved horse, my partner of so many years, across the country again, asking him to leave his all-day turnout to stand in a 12 x 24 pipe corral. He was officially a senior citizen and it didn't seem right to put him through the rigorous 2,000-mile journey again.

Selling him was out of the question. He was my heart horse and I vowed to have him until the end.

A plan sprouted in my mind. My niece Mattie also caught the horse bug early in life. She began taking lessons when she was 4 on a brown Shetland pony named Root Beer. She had even started showing in a few lead line classes. Obviously DC was too much horse for a girl of 8, both height-wise and temperament-wise, but Mattie would continue to grow and DC would continue to mellow as he aged. Perhaps there'd be a point where the two would meet and be perfect for each other.

That hope freed me to go back to California and leave DC home in Illinois. He was beloved at the boarding stable because of his dashing looks and engaging personality; I figured I would have no problem finding a suitable share boarder. Probably a teenage girl who had all the love for a horse minus the parental permission or budget for one of her own.

And so the decision was made. I would return to California and DC would remain in Illinois. I would keep him as my own, but in a sense give him away to the girls who were not me who got to ride him, groom him, and love him daily on my behalf. I hoped one day he would become Mattie's first horse. Only then could I move on.

But for the moment, I had to extend my stride forward to enlarge my world and open the doors of possibility for love. I had given Chicago my best and she gave me only memories in return.

THE REST OF the hunter course was a blur and adrenaline rush. The anticipation for the class and then the actual performance of jumping the fences with DC was a combination of nervousness and then relief when it was over. We didn't get a ribbon, but we were safe and we were fast and powerful. I had no idea this was to be the last horse show I would enjoy with Adonis.

CHAPTER 31

As American as Apple Pie?

WHEN I GOT settled in California again, this time minus a horse and with the addition of a dog, my dating life picked up again almost immediately. I perked up when I got a local match on my Internet dating site. I thought he was very handsome and he certainly was tall. He looked like he could have been an actor with high cheekbones and penetrating coffee-colored eyes. And he lived close by. He was Chinese and I was intrigued.

I began communicating with Tony (which I thought was a surprising name for a Chinese man) via email. He was clever and sweet and very fun to swap missives with. Before I got too involved via the web, I phoned my friend Jean who knows a little something about Chinese culture, as she is Chinese herself. I gave her my password and she looked over his profile and gave me her two cents.

"Susan, he's a millionaire."

He suddenly became more attractive, although I wasn't sure how she could glean this pertinent detail from merely scanning a profile. So I asked; she said to trust her. She claimed she knew her "Asian brothers," explaining if his parents brought him and his siblings over here to go to high school or attend college, they had money. "And he's going to think you're great. He'll totally go for you. You're tall. The blond hair. You're like the Western ideal."

I emailed Tony my cell phone number so we could set up a phone date. I was in for a surprise.

Tony had a very thick accent. Thick like peanut butter. Thick like cars on an L.A. freeway. My heart sank. I managed to understand him throughout most of the conversation, and only had to ask him to repeat himself a couple of times. By the end of the conversation I realized with dismay I was an accentist.

I projected into the future and thought about hearing Tony's voice with the accent say, "Good night, dear," and "I love you," and, "How was your day, Hon?" and I knew I just couldn't do it. I couldn't love a man who was hard to understand.

But he was a millionaire.

I contacted Jean again to tell her I wasn't sure about the accent. She reprimanded me and said to stop being shallow.

"Well he does like to play tennis. Maybe we have more in common than I thought."

Inspired by Jean's scolding, I had an inner dialogue with myself about judging people and what really matters is what's on the inside, not externals. The good Susan won that battle and found herself a few days later sitting in the middle of Peet's Coffee at a small round table with Tony on the other side.

In person, Tony was exactly how I thought he might

be—kind, easy to talk to, and a good listener. We had a nice chat. The accent bothered me less in person and it was easier to understand, but I did get a glimpse of his hands and thought about how delicate they looked. His fingers were slender and daintier than my own. They were actually pretty. They looked as though they had never pounded a hammer or had dirt under the nails from doing chores or yard work. I excused him, figuring if you're a millionaire, you don't have to get your hands dirty. Other people do that for you.

I had a strong hunch he was not the love of my life, but the optimist in me kept on hoping and kept asking polite get-to-know-you questions. About halfway through our date, after connecting over our mutual interest in tennis, I asked,

"So when you run, what music do you listen to?"

I nearly fell out of my chair and had to rein it in to not laugh aloud when he said, "Celine Dion and Mariah Carey."

I could never imagine a straight American guy saying such a thing! I had a flashback to the scene in the movie "How to Lose a Guy in Ten Days" where Kate Hudson intentionally tries to dump Matthew McConaughey's character. To do this she buys tickets for them to go see Celine Dion.

As the date was winding down, I couldn't shake the notion Tony was just not American enough for me to treasure like I should. I was about ready to say the obligatory, "Really nice to finally have a chance to meet you in person. Thanks for the coffee," when he sprang another date invitation on me and I had no time to react.

"There is a musical downtown L.A. Would you like going to *My Fair Lady* next week?"

I said yes. It was a knee-jerk response. I didn't have time to think of a creative excuse. He was so direct in his invitation. And besides, who wouldn't want to see *My Fair Lady*?

A few days later Tony phoned to plan the upcoming event. He apologized because he couldn't get good tickets. I assured him any tickets would be good. He was concerned we'd be too far away from the stage. I suggested taking binoculars.

The day of our second date came and Tony insisted on picking me up at my apartment. I was trying to make it more casual by suggesting I could meet him at the theater since he worked in downtown L.A. and the show was in downtown L.A. It didn't make sense to me he'd go through rush hour traffic one way to come to my home and then head back into it to go to the play. But he insisted on picking me up at my apartment.

After briefly meeting my roommate Heidi, Tony and I crossed the threshold of my loft door to begin our night on the town. Tony opened doors for me, drove sanely and remembered the binoculars.

He announced we were going to Little Tokyo for dinner before the show, and I grew apprehensive about using chopsticks in front of him. I can use chopsticks; I had vacationed in Asia before, but I was certainly no expert. I was worried I'd be doing it wrong and flashed forward to the awkwardness of being in a bicultural marriage someday.

"Honey, you need to hold the chopsticks more like

this. Oh, and please remember to remove your shoes at the door. Also my mom and dad are moving in with us."

The meal came and we weren't even offered chopsticks. The server brought us both shiny forks.

I'd like to think I'm a fairly skilled conversationalist, and it's a good thing, because at this stage, I was ready to be done with the date, but we still had the musical to attend. We finished up our meal and headed over to the theater.

Just as the *Los Angeles Times* review boasted, the production was outstanding. It was hard for me to understand Eliza Doolittle during parts of the show due to her intense cockney accent. While I was sitting there with my elbow next to Tony snugly fit between my side and the shared armrest so as to avoid bumping his elbow, I wondered if Tony could understand Eliza's cockney accent. I simultaneously prayed he wouldn't try to hold my hand or lean into me. We took turns using the binoculars even though our seats were on the main floor near the back.

The intermission came and Tony said he needed to use the restroom. I hung out in the lobby watching the couples who were on dates in which there was something going on—attraction, commonalities, sexual tension, maybe even profound friendship. I had none of that with Tony. It was like he was my event partner for the evening; he was a decent person to sit next to while enjoying a show. He returned bearing the soundtrack CD for me. I thanked him and he wished me a happy birthday. It wasn't my birthday, it was seven months away. In spite of his kindness I couldn't feign romantic interest. Even though he was a millionaire.

The show ended, and as we drove back to my apartment in virtual silence, I plotted how to make a quick escape from the car and Tony's presence. I already had enough information. The chemistry just wasn't there, and I knew it would never bloom—at least on my part. The accent wouldn't grow on me and become cuter or unnoticeable. I didn't want his girl hands touching me anywhere. Our date felt like a meeting. I was done. It only took two dates to figure it out.

Tony pulled his luxury sedan up next to my building and zipped over to open the door for me. I stepped out into the velvety night, stars overhead, crickets chirping, Tony at my side. My anxiety intensified with every step as we strolled along the sidewalk to the front door. I tried to make the farewell brief and thanked him, saying it was a nice play and goodnight. Tony leaned in to kiss me and I quickly turned my face to the side so as to fend off his romantic advance. What could have been a disastrous first and last kiss instead became a benign peck on the cheek.

Once inside my apartment, I knew I was safe. I'd never have to go on another date with Tony again. I'd never have to dodge another kiss. I already had my letting-him-down-easy email halfway composed in my brain. That was the end of it, or so I thought.

Heidi was home. "Hey how'd the date go?"

"The production was great. I just don't see myself with Tony. There was no chemistry. He's so sweet, but I can't get over the accent and his girl hands. And this might sound bad, but I don't think he's American enough."

"I know! I noticed his hands. I thought I might crush his hand when I shook it."

The next day I got a voicemail from Tony; I heard him asking about Binaca. Why was he calling about a breath freshening spray?

After listening to the message again, I realized he was calling about his *binoculars* I had offered to carry in my oversized purse. I forgot to give them back to him! I had to see him again to return the binoculars. And I had to somehow let him know this was not a relationship meant to be. I dreaded both tasks like the last day of a vacation.

I composed and clicked send on the following email:

Hi Tony,

How are you?

I wanted to thank you for taking me to the musical. That was a fantastic production and I had a good time. And it was thoughtful of you to surprise me with the CD. I know I'll listen to it.

Anyway, internet dating is such a bittersweet experience because I've met some really great people—you're one of them. I know you're on the website with the intention of finding the right fit for your life. For me, I don't see the friendship we've struck up turning into a romantic relationship. The chemistry isn't there.

I think you're quite a gentleman and have a lot to

offer the right woman. I wish you all the best in your search. It's been a pleasure to get to know you and thank you for making the effort to get to know me.

By the way, let me know how I can get the binoculars to you. I'd be happy to drop them off at your house or meet you somewhere for the exchange. Let me know what you prefer.

Sincerely,
Susan

I received a very gracious response.

It is sad to learn the truth, to realize you do not feel the same way to me as I do to you. Too bad, I thought we could have a tennis match in this coming weekend or next week. I thought we could have something together in the future, but obviously, I am wrong. No matter what, it is still my pleasure to get to know you. You are a very sweet lady and a sincere and nice person. I do enjoy the time being with you. Whoever can capture your heart will be a lucky guy for sure.

Anyhow, I think I need to review my Chemistry textbook to see how to make better chemistry. I don't believe love in first sight myself.

I wrote back.

I wish relational chemistry were something that could be worked on by referring to a book, but alas, that is not the case. I guess that's part of the magic and mystery of relationships. I've been on both sides of the "there's no chemistry" equation and neither one is fun. It just is. Thank you for your kind words.

I recounted the whole awkward scenario to my friend Dana who volunteered to be my wingman in returning the binoculars. I was thrilled. The plan I forged was to drop the binoculars off on my way home from a Cinco de Mayo party on Saturday. It wouldn't really require a special trip—it was kind of a breezy way of seeing him again.

A few days later, Dana and I made it to the party a tad on the late side. There were more people in attendance than the hosts thought would show, so we both had a meager serving of tortilla chip fragments and bean dip scrapings from the sides of the dish. We mixed and mingled and then had to leave to run the uncomfortable binocular errand.

I phoned Tony from my car and his voice came on like a loudspeaker over the Bluetooth connection. He gave me his address. I hadn't heard of the street, but it was no problem as I immediately put the numbers into my GPS. When we hung up, I looked to Dana to validate the accent was kind of a turn off and I was still an okay person. She said I was good and added she thought she knew the street and if she was right, the house was located near the Huntington Gardens, a very upscale neighborhood.

His house was about a 15 minute drive from our party. The closer we got to it, the more winding the streets became and the houses were further spaced apart, enormous and regal like the homes along the Clampetts' street in *The Beverly Hillbillies.*

The GPS voice alerted, "Destination," and I steered my Jeep into the arched driveway in front of a two-story mansion outlined with layers of boxwood and giant topiaries. An ornate fountain of a large crane graced the front lawn in the line of the front door. I stifled a surprised laugh. Dana and I got out of the car and tried to keep it together as though all our friends lived in homes like that and this was just a routine errand.

I rang the doorbell and wondered if a butler would appear. Instead, a minute later, Tony opened the door with a quiet smile. I said hello, introduced Dana, and handed over the binoculars. Tony warmly insisted we come in.

Dana and I stepped into the marble foyer, which was the same size as my entire apartment. We exchanged niceties for a few minutes. He asked how the party was. I said it was good, but the hosts hadn't planned on so many people coming and they ran out of food. He insisted we come into the kitchen. *Why did I have to share that fact?*

This was not going to be a quick drop off.

We followed him. "Would you like something to eat? You must be hungry." I said I was all right, but thanked him anyway. I didn't want to belabor the return of the binoculars. He then opened the refrigerator and produced an apple pie. "Are you sure you don't want some apple pie? It's really good. Marie Callender's."

Dana declined, but I just couldn't say no to apple pie. And I was still hungry.

As I sat in the middle of his sleek stainless steel and granite kitchen, surrendering to the slice of apple pie, I pondered the irony of my not wanting to be with Tony because he wasn't American enough, yet here he was with an apple pie.

Dana meanwhile was the perfect wing[man]woman. She carried on a conversation about her native New Orleans and what the difference is between Cajun and Creole people and cooking. Tony seemed interested, having never been to the South. After about 15 minutes of awkwardness masked by Dana's healthy chatter, we were able to bid Tony farewell and goodnight.

Dana and I exited the columned front entry of what could have been my new home and wordlessly got into the car. Once the doors were closed we simultaneously erupted into giggles and I told Dana to not say anything until we were out of the driveway. I started the engine and put the car into drive as Dana said, "Whatever you do, don't run over the birds!" referring to the regal fountain.

Once I made it down the block a bit I moaned, "Dana! What am I going to do? Isn't he sweet? He's such a nice guy. And that house. Am I being stupid? There's just no chemistry. Do you think it could develop over time? Maybe I should reconsider?"

"Girl, that would be one cold, lonely house! I think you need hot love in a shack somewhere instead of no chemistry in a marble mansion. Don't settle."

I didn't want him, but I wanted him to find a nice girlfriend, not someone who'd want him for his money. A sweet girl who would appreciate his accent and his hands. As we drove home, Dana and I wracked our brains and offered up names of friends who might possibly be a good fit for Tony. We couldn't come up with any suitable women for him.

A few days later, I recounted my short-lived romance with Tony to my friend Martin. He assured me Tony was in good shape, "Don't worry about him. He's got money. Some women go for that. He'll have no problem at all finding someone." I hoped it was true.

Several days passed and I kept thinking about Tony, the apple pie, all that glorious marbled space for one solitary man. I concluded until Tony could find a nice girl, he should get a rescue dog in the interim. We all need somebody to love.

Finally my curiosity about Tony's house (that could have been mine) got the best of me. I knew there was no future for us, but I just HAD to know more about what could have been. I had never in all my life been invited in to such grandeur. There was no harm in just dropping his address into Zillow to see the aerial view and home value, right? (I guess I didn't listen too well to Jean's admonishment to not be shallow).

I inserted the address of Tony's house into the data fields and was astounded to see the house had seven bedrooms and nine baths. The photo showed not only a pool in the backyard, but a tennis court! So *that's* where we could have had his proposed tennis match. This was too much! After this discovery, for some reason I had to email the link with the picture of the colossal home and incredible yard with the pool and tennis court to my family members.

My mom's return email said, "Dad says, next time you have to return binoculars, we'll do it."

CHAPTER 32

Happy Feet Balboa

IN THE SUMMER of 2008, Shelly, my Paris traveling companion and I decided to jaunt off for a girls' weekend getaway to Montreal. It was a cheaper, closer alternative to Paris, only about two and a half hours by plane from Chicago and still very French. At this life stage Shelly had two young kids at home, so a European vacation was out of the question. I did not suspect that I would find romance in a Montreal Internet cafe one muggy afternoon.

Before our trip I had flown to Chicago and spent time with my parents, sister, niece, and my beautiful DC. He was doted on by a number of girls and women at the barn. Every day he was turned out in a field with one pony and a dark horse named Gandhi. Without fail, when I would walk over to the gate and call his name, he would lift his head high, perk his ears my direction and then with his head low and relaxed, stroll over to me dolloping heavy breaths near my hands where I usually had a carrot for him.

DC didn't hold it against me that I moved away from him—that I gave him up to make a happier life for myself. Meanwhile I had found a highly-trained dressage horse to shareboard in Pasadena so I could get my horse itch scratched as a California resident.

It just wasn't the same.

I had temporarily given up on the online dating scene. Granted, I had met a number of fine individuals like the veterinarian from Indianapolis. In lieu of flowers, he brought a dog toy for Winnie, which I found very sweet. There was also the retina surgeon from Iowa who had a great sense of humor and was very humble. I wanted to like him because I respected him as a person; that special spark was just not present. It all boiled down to one question: do I want him to kiss me? If the answer was no, then I probably should save time for both of us and end things early.

The guy I met in the Internet cafe by way of the computer screen was very handsome with an athletic build and short, dark hair. His digital image smiled up at me. His screen name was Happy Feet.

I had been a fairly active participant on a particular Christian dating site a few years earlier. However, after excessive messages from foreign men claiming they knew I was a "sweet lady" whom God wanted them pursue, men who looked like my dad's contemporaries, and manly men passionate about the NRA, I decided to throw in the towel. At least temporarily. After months of inactivity, I received an offer for two weeks free as the site was trying to lure me back for only $19.95 a month. The optimist/romantic in me decided to give it another shot. So in between sightseeing and dining, I found myself sitting in a Montreal café cubicle, checking email and my Internet dating account, just to see what/who was out there.

I logged in with low expectations, but reminded myself I knew at least three normal people who had met their spouses online. Amy, at whose wedding I'd been a bridesmaid, a co-worker, and the daughter of another co-worker. I had proof Internet dating worked for some people, and reasoned maybe it would work for me.

I had selected "Balboa" as my online dating screen name in reference to the swing dance I had set out to learn a few years earlier and had really enjoyed, even though I had not mastered it. As I logged in, a notification from Happy Feet awaited me.

His message was short and hinted he knew how I had chosen my username—that he was a fellow swing dancer. He asked if I wanted to serve people and experience God's adventures together. It certainly was forward, but at the same time, compelling. Confidence is an attractive quality in a man.

His three profile pictures intrigued me. The first one showed him flanked by two kids, a teenage-ish boy and a little blonde girl. They sported great smiles and looked like the all-American family—people you'd want to live next door to you. I assumed they were his actual children since they resembled him, and not some random kids helping him create a staged photo op to show he loved children. The dating cyberworld had its share of wackos who did exactly that kind of thing.

I looked over his stats which revealed he was aged 41-45, around 6 feet 2 inches tall and weighed 170-185 lbs. He was divorced and had two kids, was smart, and had above average good looks (I could tell that from the picture!) and *he was a teacher*, just like me!

I quickly scanned his lengthy written profile. It was novel length and more than I could digest in a pay-by-the minute Internet session. I sent him a brief message to acknowledge the communication and thought I'd have to probe this one a bit more when I had the time (after Montreal) after I made it back to California. I was staying in Illinois with my parents for a couple more weeks during my summer vacation anyway.

The communication gave me a little extra spring in my step as we toured the rest of Montreal eating one too many crepes.

In mid August, my girlfriend Carolyn and I drove the 2,000 miles back to L.A. so I could begin my new school year. Meanwhile Happy Feet, a.k.a. Mark, and I exchanged a few short emails. I wasn't sure what to make of him since he was eight years older than me, his profile was so long and "open" (on the site he stated he preferred women who had small butts—I couldn't help but wonder if I fell into that category or not), and I had never dated someone with kids.

Once I made it back home to L.A. I showed his pictures to Heidi, "He's cute and sounds nice. You *have* to go out with him! Give this one a chance."

I emailed Happy Feet my phone number and shortly thereafter had a phone conversation lasting two and a half hours, in which he spelled out his life story in intricate detail from his lonely childhood in an alcoholic home, to running away to his aunt's as a teenager, to the sad demise of his 17-year marriage. I lay on my scarlet duvet cover, Motorola Razr in hand, taking it all in.

I tend to be a more private, introverted person, and while taking in all this new information I kept wondering if he was oversharing. I was also a bit taken aback there wasn't more give and take, with him asking questions to get to know me. My uneasiness abated when, as we said our goodbyes, Mark revealed he wanted to tell me his whole story because he figured if he were a single woman potentially getting involved with a divorced man, he'd want to know what had happened. I felt more at ease.

My cell phone rang two days later as Mark was house sitting for his uncle at the beach in Dana Point—too far for me to drive on a weeknight from Glendale. Instead of having a live, in-person date, we had another phone date. I did more of the talking this time. I wanted to just meet him and get it over with, as I was uncertain whether he was as awesome and sweet as I thought he might be, or if he was a kook. It would be better to know sooner rather than later.

My first day back at school, the last week in August, was filled with meetings. Mark called to let me know he was going mountain biking, but the plans changed and he just happened to be near my neighborhood, visiting his former in-laws. He could get together with me that night. I had a church volunteers meeting to go to after work so I told him we could meet, but it would have to be later, after the dinner hour. He said not to worry; he'd go over to 24 Hour Fitness and workout while he waited for me.

As I neared my apartment building after the church tutoring ministry party, Mark called to say he was in town and ready to meet me; he was finished with the gym and good to go.

Oh crap! I'm not even ready. Where should I meet him? What can we do? Since I was technically the local, I thought it was on me to orchestrate our meetup. He suggested getting together at the Americana, an outdoor shopping mall, appropriately open and public.

I rushed upstairs to my apartment and quickly freshened up to avoid the shiny, end-of-day glow. I sported flip flops, jeans and a blue empire waist T-shirt. I didn't really have time for full-on first date primping. Besides, I had low expectations based on the numerous other Internet dates I had been on. I was fairly confident this one wouldn't be any different, but at least I could gain more material for my book of bad dates.

On my way out the door I walked past my dog curled up on her brown cushy bed and thought I should probably take her with me. I figured dogs have a sixth sense about people. If my date were a bad man, Winnie would save me. Surely he wouldn't try any funny business with a watchful, 70-pound Doberman at my side.

About a half hour after his call, I pulled my Jeep Liberty into a slanted parking spot, a couple of blocks from the shopping and wondered if this was going to be a big waste of time. Winnie trotted as I walked down the mostly-deserted sidewalk.

A tall, tan, muscular man in a sleeveless white tennis shirt and white shorts started walking in my direction and I was trying hard not to grin at the mere sight of him. "Susan, it's what's on the inside that counts," I chided myself. But I had always thought tennis players were sexy. He looked like he'd just arrived from Wimbledon. He didn't look sweaty—just sporty and hot.

"Well, hello Dear," I shook his hand, looked into his bright blue eyes and the rest was a blur. He bent over to pet and talk to Winnie and she wagged her stubby tail in a gesture of hospitable approval. We had both already eaten dinner and Mark was not a coffee drinker and we had a dog, so our options for the date were pretty limited. We strolled past the upscale boutiques and bantered about our day. About five minutes into our date, a uniformed security guard approached me to say my dog was not allowed there.

"But I've seen other dogs around," I complained like a whiny child, "everyone else gets to; it's not fair." He said it was a breed-specific restriction. I didn't argue, but thought about how ridiculous the rule was and how wrong the stereotype about Dobermans is.

"I can run back and put her in your car," Mark volunteered. I said I would go with him, thinking even though I was sure he was most likely a decent person, I didn't want some strange man to have my car keys AND my precious dog! His chivalrous offer did not go unnoticed, nor did his well-defined biceps.

We ambled back to the mall and spotted a Pinkberry frozen yogurt shop. Mark deferred to me for placing the order. I asked for a vanilla with chocolate chips and two spoons. Mark stepped forward and paid the cashier saying, "We're on a first date. We just met on the Internet." A younger version of me would have been mortified at this revelation. The seasoned Internet dater version of me just rolled with the comment. I could tell my date was a character and it made him all the more appealing.

We sat in the shop talking and eating. Even though he was a math teacher, he had an English teacher's vocabulary. And he was funny. He had confidence and was a great storyteller. He was way more interesting than all the previous men I had met on the Internet. Soon I was deeply enthralled with my new love interest.

Mark.

Mark and Susan. It sounded pretty good together in my head. He was a *teacher* and swing dancer. *And* a tennis player. How could this be? He was too good to be true. Would he really go for me? I hoped I wasn't getting set up for another round of unrequited "like."

I thought back to a friend in Chicago who was a single gal for many years. I lost touch with her, and when we reunited due to a chance meeting, I found out she was newly engaged. We met a week later for tacos to catch up and swap stories. She had met the man of her dreams, the answer to her prayers, literally. My friend had taken her husband need very seriously and presented her request to the Lord.

She had prayed her future spouse would be tall (she was a tall girl, maybe 5'10-11"), have brown hair, blue eyes, and own a boat (because she loved boating, but didn't have the money or connections to pursue that hobby). Well, she was thrilled to tell me her husband-to-be met all the criteria she had asked God for. I wasn't so sure that was the way to go in talking to God about my desire for a future husband. I didn't want to be like the spoiled kid telling Santa what she wanted.

Over the years I had prayed something to this effect: Lord, please help me to find a man who is devoted to You and head over heels for me. You know what's best for me, but it would be really cool if he were a teacher too. And a swing dancer. And played tennis.

I also added on a part asking God if and when I would meet that man, he (the man) would know sooner rather than later. That it would be obvious to both of us we were meant for each other and there wouldn't be any long, dragged out period of "hanging out" in which he would deliberate my merit and then decide I wasn't worthy. My heart couldn't handle another hang out relationship like the bad and ultimately embarrassing Shane experience.

Could it be like my friend in Chicago, my prayers were actually being answered in the way I hoped? Was this charming math teacher the man meant for me?

When we left Pinkberry, we paused for a while next to the large, lighted fountain in the center of the mall. Mark commented on how he had no idea Glendale was so nice. He was very impressed with the city. The fountain would periodically shoot a spray of dazzling water, like a mini-Bellagio. Frank Sinatra crooned over the mall sound system.

I looked up noticing the strands of white lights zig-zagging across the plaza. It hit me right then this was indeed a romantic destination. Without trying to set up the situation, I invited Mark to this dreamy venue. As we sat next to the fountain chatting, Mark complimented my looks and I wondered if he would try to kiss me. Unlike so many previous dates where I thought, "Oh! I hope he doesn't kiss me," this time I thought how nice it would be if our lips met. I was ready.

He apparently wasn't. We began to walk back to my car and he said he really enjoyed meeting me, but I should know he was dating other people. I suspected he had just given me a polite brush off. We exchanged a cordial hug, said good-bye and I got back in my Jeep, wondering if I'd ever see the handsome, sweet teacher again.

Little did I know I had just been on my last first date!

CHAPTER 33

As the Violins Played

"GEORGE, I'D LIKE to introduce you to my girlfriend Susan. Susan, this is George,"

I stood next to Mark near the top of the hillside as we waited for the Pacific Symphony Orchestra to begin playing Tchaikovsky. Date number two was at Mark's local swing dance studio where I was relieved to have him introduce me not just to other women, but to other men too. One of the thoughts that entered my mind was a dance studio, no matter how tame the dance form (not Dirty Dancing or Lambada), could be a prime place to use to pick up people. By having Mark introduce me to men as well as women, it showed me he was friendly—he genuinely loved to dance and was invested in getting to know everyone in the community—not just the pretty girls. That spoke volumes about his character.

The concert was our third date and it came about in kind of a friendly challenge as we talked on the phone.

"You don't like orchestras, do you? Like enough to go to a concert?" Mark asked.

Was this a trap? If I said yes I could sound highbrow, if I said no I could sound uncultured.

I sought out the middle ground, "I do. In fact, I've been to orchestra performances before. Do you think people from the Midwest don't like classical music?"

"Well I just wasn't sure if that's what you were into. So there's this concert coming up at the Pacific Amphitheater—it's Tchaikovsky—and I thought I could take you to it—if that's your thing. We could bring a picnic."

At the mention of a picnic I was in. Standing next to Mark with the large fleece blanket as he held our romantic picnic dinner of veggie lasagna, chili and cornbread and being introduced as his girlfriend was exhilarating.

We found a spot not far from the friend, but not so close it would be awkward, and began to butter our cornbread as the strings warmed up. I wondered if the blanket would get grass stains as it was cream colored.

As we ended the meal, Mark produced a piece of folder printer paper and said he had a poem for me. Just as he was about to read it, the lights went out on the seating area and brightly shone on stage. Mark shot me a grin and refolded his paper.

My blue-jeaned knee touched Mark's thigh as we shared the chili from the same to-go container. The music kept coming—swarms of notes from drum and viola, cymbals and flute. We sat side by side holding hands. About 45 minutes into the grand musical numbers, we began to fidget. Even with the comfort of each other to lean into, going from cross-legged to a less extreme version of a yoga seated twist pose, it became increasingly uncomfortable to be seated on the cold, hard ground, even with the thick blanket.

"Are you enjoying this?" Mark asked.

"Yes. What about you?"

"Yes," he said.

After a pause I offered, "If you want to go, we can go. Maybe there's something else we can do."

"You're the coolest date ever!" he burst out.

"I mean I like the music, but I'm not *that* into classical music and after a while it all starts sounding very similar. I've enjoyed what I've heard so far."

Mark continued to smile as he rounded up the picnic items and plopped them back into the bag. As we stood up he grabbed the cream blanket, shook it out and hoisted it together into a haphazard rectangle. We picked our way through the scattered blankets of the crowd and headed back to his SUV at a quicker pace than when we had arrived.

Mark drove the twisting road to Laguna Beach, where he parked and again pulled out the mysterious paper. The light in his car's interior stayed on for a few seconds as he unfolded the paper.

"And now for some plagiarized poetry for you." I smirked, uncomfortable with such an emotional overture. Just as he smiled and took a deep breath, about to read the love poetry, the light went out in his car and he joked about how difficult it was to share his deeply thoughtful, plagiarized poems.

After the in-car poetry reading during which I giggled nervously, we ambled up and down the sidewalks along the shops and boutiques on Highway 1. Loud music throbbed as we walked past a club and lights twinkled in the windows of a high-end restaurant. Svelte, high-heeled women with unnaturally straight and shiny hair passed us arm and arm with their dates. Mark's attention stayed fixed on me.

"You know, I was really attracted to you through your writing. I like the way you expressed yourself on your dating profile."

"You're quite a writer yourself—your profile," I laughed referencing his epic-length bio on the dating site. "Not bad for a math guy."

"I just wanted to be up front—to weed out the incompatible ones."

"You know, I've been on so many bad dates I started writing about them. I took a memoir class last year. There was this one blind date I went on years ago where the guy got pulled over and he didn't have insurance, current tags or a valid driver's license!"

"Really?!"

"It wasn't funny then, but it is now."

"Maybe I'll give you a reason to stop writing," he grinned.

From our sidewalk stroll, we made our way down a stairwell leading to the beach. The damp air pressed my face and a few minutes later, after a flirtatious conversation, Mark's lips pressed against my lips. The waves crashed nearby as my heart soared.

As each month passed over the next year, Mark and I grew closer. So close, in fact, we got the name of a counselor who specialized in pre-marital and blended family therapy, from a friend of a friend. Week after week for several months, we spent 50 minutes pouring out who we were to the counselor and each other, unboxing our fears and insecurities. We knew the statistics for second marriage success, which were not particularly successful. We wanted a heads-up on the struggles we would most likely encounter and tools to power through them. Ultimately, we wanted a green light on our union from an unbiased source.

Much like a set of X-rays taken during a pre-purchase exam for a new horse, we both dutifully filled out a premarital survey/assessment. The final counseling session's purpose was to have the therapist illuminate the questions we answered differently enough to have contrasting opinions, that way we could talk them through. We already knew of our personality differ-ences—Mark is an extrovert, while I'm an introvert, and how we use time. One of us likes to be early, the other rushes around and is last-minute, I won't say who.

At the end of the session the counselor smiled, pro-claiming that based on the data, he felt we had a high likelihood of having both a satisfying and happy mar-riage. We passed the test! And so we continued dating with a greater purpose in mind than just the next deli-cious meal at a fun restaurant.

It finally seemed like the bridal path I was on was bridal with an "a," not an "e."

CHAPTER 34

One Last Big Purchase

"LET'S GO OUT for dinner this Thursday. I really want to see you. Need to see you."

Why on earth did Mark want me to drive down to Orange County on a weeknight? Everyone knows L.A. traffic is about the worst in the nation, possibly universe. Frustrated commuters sat on the 5 Freeway like a giant parking lot.

He was so insistent, I agreed to go along with the plan and prepared myself for the long drive, which would be stop and go with mostly stops.

I was in love.

Mark greeted me at the door of his apartment with a hug and a kiss and soon we set off in his Acura SUV along the winding path of Laguna Canyon Road. Nearing the coast, a white restaurant of Mexican architectural style came into view. I had never been to this restaurant, Las Brisas, before.

As the hostess showed us to our booth, Mark explained the intent was we would have a view overlooking the Pacific and sunset sky. The maddening Los Angeles traffic foiled his plan.

Mark ordered the maple-glazed salmon and asked to swap out the fingerling potatoes with mashed potatoes, and I ordered the chicken with mango mole. We shared stories about our students and discussed the weekend's plan, which included swing dancing.

When the server came with the check, Mark reached into his pocket and winced.

"I don't have my wallet. Do you have a credit card with you? I'll pay you back."

I pulled out my gray Visa card and joked I knew where he lived and so he'd better pay me back.

After I signed the white slip of paper and tucked the pen back inside the small folder, Mark picked up my hand and said I had to see the view—that this restaurant had a great vantage point at the cliff. As we stepped outside into the the black cloak of night, there really was no view of the Pacific. However, the damp air carried the unmistakable beach smell—a soft fusion of salt and earth. It was pungent and organic and sweet. The swishing waves pulsed and receded. Even though we couldn't see them, the majestic waters proclaimed their existence.

Mark extended his arm to me as we navigated down steep concrete stairs. "This can be very romantic. Or dangerous," he chuckled nervously. "Let's just sit here."

Shoulder touching shoulder, midway down the steps, Mark reached into the pocket of his black leather jacket and produced a homemade card.

"I wrote you a poem." He held up his Blackberry so

the glow of the device allowed me to see a picture of us smiling, arms around each other.

"Is this one of those plagiarized poems like you read at the symphony?" I smiled and began to read it silently.

To my Dearest Susan,
Winnie knew best, when we met that first night.
I saw her wink and suggest I take a bite!
Looked at your lips . . . I was checking you out!
Laguna's next week; here comes a drought.

You think I'm a kook, will I get to bat?
One day at Porto's my advances fell flat!
U2 concert? That would do the trick!

Make her think I'm Bono; lay it on thick!
Alas I chose Tchaikovsky—(not very bright),
Read into your comments, which led to that night.
Recited poetry—to soften your defense!
You giggled like a schoolgirl. No horse sense.

My final weapon, a walk on the beach . . .
Eager prey, you were within reach!

So now I want my minx forever,
On to just horse stories found so clever.
Out with internet dates gone awry, on to
New adventures from God's great supply.

I love you Susan,
This is my acrostic gift to you.

At first because of the bad lighting and the tiny, fancy script font, I thought the line read: "This is my sarcastic gift to you." Then I re-read the word and realized it said *acrostic*.

It didn't seem possible, but the words were literally spelled out in front of me, the first letter of each line of the poem contained the not-so-secret message: Will you marry me soon?

"Yes, of course!" I leaned into this man I had held out for literally for decades. His muscular arm drew me in to a sweet, seated side hug and our lips met once again. As our faces drew apart I could feel my smile. *He loves me. He wants to marry me. Me!*

My reverie was broken by Mark's joyful cry, "Now I'll get a tax break! Yes!"

He had forgotten his wallet, but he didn't forget this special gift. My love produced a brown velvet box my mom had given to him when we visited my parents' home the previous Christmas. I opened the small present and a familiar gem sparkled at me: an Edwardian shaped round diamond I had inherited. This glittery ring had been my great-grandmother's whom I had never met.

Prior to the holidays, I told Mark I didn't want him spending money on an engagement ring when I'd rather have another horse for an engagement gift. One native to California and with no memory of the expansive fields of the Midwest. A younger horse, not to replace DC, but complement him. I knew it would take some time, but I was okay with it.

"WHERE'S MARK?" I asked.

"I last saw him napping in the hammock," my sister Linda said.

While Mark dozed in a hammock under the shade of my friend Diane's tree that July afternoon, the royal treatment was bestowed on me up in her master bathroom.

It was one of those hot and humid Midwest days, the kind compelling folks not from the Midwest question how people can live in such a very cold place that also gets so incredibly hot. And sticky.

With a makeup artist-finessed face and hair styled like the 1940s siren Veronica Lake, I slipped into my fitted lace gown—the first wedding dress I had tried on on a whim, five months earlier.

My co-workers and I had just enjoyed dinner at Roy's Hawaiian fusion restaurant. Across the street on Colorado Boulevard in Pasadena was a bridal boutique. Someone asked if I had been dress shopping yet, and I said no. "Let's go check out the dresses across the street!"

So the five of us entered the shop and one of my friends gushed, "This is our friend the bride. She'd love to try on some dresses." I was kind of embarrassed, but played along.

"What type of dress are you envisioning?"

"Something kind of vintage looking, and not big and poofy."

The saleswoman nodded, walked away and came back presenting a gorgeous ivory gown.

"Do you like this?"

"Yes! That's really pretty. I'll try it."

The moment I zipped up and stepped out of the dressing room, a chorus of ooohhs greeted me. The consensus was the wedding dress was gorgeous and perfect for me. For as long and difficult as it was to find my groom, it was a short and easy process to find my wedding gown. I shopped for a few more weeks at different stores just to see what else was out there, but came back to Gown Number One.

PLANNING AN OUT-OF-STATE wedding was one thing, but planning how to coordinate life with a horse, and a husband, and two adolescent stepchildren was something else entirely. And why not throw in a 1980s fixer-upper house to make things interesting?

When I had last returned to Illinois to consult with the wedding florist and find a caterer, I had noticed some changes in DC's back due to age. I realized his saddle no longer fit him properly. He had been such a trooper of a horse—my best friend—and I knew I owed it to him to buy a new saddle so he would live out his days in comfort no matter who was riding him.

I assumed only another horse person would understand why I'd want to buy a new saddle for an old horse. So a week before my wedding, in the midst of working out details with the caterer, photographer and DJ, I had a saddle fitter from the local tack shop bring out a lineup of saddles to test on my beloved.

The winning option fit DC almost like it was custom-built for his Thoroughbred withers and aging back. I thought it was pretty and comfy, so I wrote a check for my last big purchase as a single woman.

Mark was a frugal guy and it didn't make sense to bring a discussion of something only a horse person would understand into our new union as a potential point of conflict.

MY GIRLFRIENDS MET me at the base of Diane's grand staircase and gave me tight hugs with tears as I met my dad. Although it was a backyard wedding, he bought a new tan suit for the occasion. Although I know he hated wearing a tie, he looked amazing—a little like the actor James Woods. We walked arm in arm across the lawn to a white arbor festooned with pink and yellow flowers, and there my long-awaited groom waited for me. I have never felt more special and loved in my whole life. My mom beamed in her dark blue dress, and my sisters and their families were all there dressed to the nines. The familiar faces of cousins and close friends flanked the aisleway.

I was so happy I couldn't cry. I was floating.

When Pastor Chuck, a long-time family friend, read the lines of the vows for us to repeat, Mark choked up and tears streamed down his face. My heart melted even more and I squeezed both of his hands a little tighter. Clouds started to mottle what had been a dazzling blue sky. The air temperature dropped noticeably and just as the pastor declared, "By the powers vested in me by the state of Illinois, I now proclaim you husband and wife," a distant, ominous rumble in the sky made for a dramatic effect. Mark and I and some of our guests giggled.

The photographer rallied all of the attendees to one side of the yard for a group shot. As soon as the photo was taken, the skies opened, and we all made a beeline to the tent. For the next 15 minutes, a pleasant summer shower lingered—a late, but not unwelcome wedding guest. As the rain petered out, a brilliant rainbow showed off in the sky, a message of hope.

Just as the first recorded rainbow sighting by Noah symbolized a covenant and promise, deep down I knew this wedding day rainbow was not a simple coincidence.

CHAPTER 35

Too Soon for Goodbye

THERE'S NO EASY way to slip into life in a blended family, but sometimes in real life, like in riding, you just have to keep your eyes up and keep moving forward. And breathe.

My new identity as a wife and stepmom was difficult to navigate, and my familiar identity, the one tied up in my beloved horse—my true better half—was 2,000 miles away. A reunion of DC and me seemed nearly impossible.

Four months into my marriage, just as I was attempting to find a suitable boarding location for DC, the rug was pulled out from under me in one 4 a.m. phone call.

When the trill of my cell phone alarm woke me at 5:30, I noticed a missed call and retrieved the voicemail. The barn manager in Illinois said DC was sick and she had had to call the vet and that I should call her back.

I dialed the number as soon as I got the message. I didn't catch on right away how grave the situation was. I thanked the manager for getting the vet and for calling to let me know.

"He's not looking very good. Something's off," she said. "I trailered him here to the hospital. I will have you talk to Dr. _____." I had no idea who the veterinarian was, and I didn't quite catch her name. She sounded young.

With my phone at my ear, I walked out to the family room and threw the blanket from our sofa over my shoulders. Mark was seated watching an early-morning financial market TV show.

The veterinarian slowly walked me through DC's symptoms and what she had done to try to help him and then gave me my options—there were only two—surgery, or the one no one should ever have to entertain.

My mind raced. Since I was so far geographically removed and sensed true compassion and competence from this stranger on the other end 2,000 miles away, the words rolled off my tongue instinctively, "If he were your horse, what would you do?"

This can't be real! I just haven't found the right situation for DC here in California. He's supposed to live here—with me.

"I'm really sorry," she stated slowly. "But I would euthanize. His system is already compromised and to do a surgery, it would be $8,000 just to get him on the table. I'm not sure he would be able to handle the anaesthesia. He's an older horse."

I couldn't speak.

Only four months earlier I was told by my veterinarian DC was the picture of health—that he didn't know he was 23, and to keep riding him and working him. And he would be healthy enough for a cross-country trailer ride. This had to be a mistake. Myriad thoughts burst through my brain and yet it was simultaneously blank.

"He's a Thoroughbred, right?"

"Yes," I barely breathed.

"Well, you've given him a great life. You should feel good about that. You know, it doesn't always end up that way for Thoroughbreds."

I didn't know what this young veterinarian was saying about *other* Thoroughbreds, but I knew exactly what she was saying about *my* Thoroughbred.

I swallowed and then reluctantly gave my verbal approval. The weight of an anvil pressed on my heart.

Mark stood by my shoulder during the course of this conversation. When I ended the call he enveloped me with his arms as the tears escaped my eyes and coursed down my cheeks.

"I don't know what to do now."

I meant that in both the immediate—*Am I supposed to go to work?* and in the overall realm of life. It's hard to go from horse owner and equestrian to former horse owner and non-practicing equestrian.

"I think you need to go to work. There's nothing you can do here to change things." I felt his jawline rest on my cheekbone as I continued hugging him. It was as if as long as I held him and could feel the thumping pulse within Mark's chest, it would keep DC's heart beating.

I wept as I drove north on the 5 Freeway, the sun tentatively peeking over the edge of the mountains. I felt alone and dreaded sharing this devastating news with my family and friends. I knew in each retelling of the unwelcome, pre-dawn phone call with the empathetic yet frank veterinarian I had never met, I would experience the loss anew.

DC wasn't just my horse. He belonged to all the people who loved me and the riders who loved him—my niece, mom, sisters, childhood best friend Gail, the teens at the barn, and his most recent share boarder.

Mine was just the first in a string of hearts to break that November morning.

I gave up my heart horse once to pursue a brighter relational future for myself. That was only supposed to be temporary. I found my life partner in human form, and now had lost my horse partner who had been there for me for 16 years of my singleness.

I held my emotions at bay during Period 1 English, then Period 2 History. I smiled a fake smile at students and went through the motions of teaching. The ache in my heart did not subside, but lifted a little bit when I divulged my tragic secret to a fellow horse lover—another teacher at my school who grew up with horses. I am not one to embrace my colleagues, but when he hugged me it was a message from one horse lover to another: I understand your loss and pain. Sharing my secret with one person made it easier to tell another, and so I confided in the co-teacher who came to my classroom later that day. She was not a horse person.

"I'm so sorry. Go. I will cover the rest of your classes. It's okay. Just leave."

The rest of the day was gray with the exception of

dinner. It was a custody night, and Mark suggested the four of us should head out to a nice restaurant. Before our Mexican dill rice and burritos arrived on the table he prayed, thanking God for the wonderful horse DC had been and asked my heart would be healed and comforted.

God answered Mark's prayer—like all the others—but not right away.

I seem to have a history of life events only occurring in slow motion.

CHAPTER 36

Saddle Seeks Horse

A FEW DAYS after DC's death, I had the urge to write an obituary and share it with everyone who had known my horse over the years. I carefully composed a group email to spread the sad news.

Hello Friends,

This week I am mourning the loss of a great friend/awesome horse of 16 years, DC. He was the light of my life and a source of joy to so many people—my mom, sister Linda, niece, shareboarder, friend Gail, and so many more friends and horse lovers who met him throughout the years in both IL and CA.

On Monday I made the hard decision for DC to be put down as a result of injuries he received from choking.

He was taken to an equine hospital to see if a colic surgery would be an option—the initial diagnosis by the vet who came to the barn was that he colicked. When the hospital vet assessed him, she said he had choked on something (she didn't know what—maybe a wad of hay) and it had gotten into his lungs—that was the real problem, which somehow lead to the colic. The vet said she wasn't optimistic he could handle the anesthesia to perform the colic surgery and his various systems were not functioning well due to the stress of the choking. I asked her what she would do if he were her horse—she said it was such a hard decision to make, but she would have put him down.

The Tower Hill Farm barn manager Carrie, the person who called me at 3:45 a.m. Monday, had trailered him to the hospital to see if surgery was an option. Carrie lives at and runs the barn and knows DC. She agreed with me euthanasia was the right decision. She said DC didn't outwardly seem to be in any pain and he was very stoic—not his normal personality. While driving the 5 freeway in the dark, on the way to work, tears streaming down my face, I told Carrie to tell him I loved him and he had been such a good boy. With tears in her voice she said she would.

When I bought him I remember feeling guilty I was depleting my savings account to buy a horse—it seemed so extravagant. A woman at my first job gave me a piece of advice when I shared with her my tentativeness. She said, "Susan, my best friend just died of breast cancer and she was only 40. I think you should buy that horse and enjoy every minute you have with him. Life is short."

And so I did. And I have now just turned 40 myself.

My trainer Joanne "found" DC for me and nudged me to buy him when I wasn't really interested in getting a horse, as I was happily shareboarding one. I'm so grateful I did make the plunge! My mom gave me the $3,750 I needed to pay for half of DC. She always wanted a horse when she was a girl.

Through career changes and relational ups and downs, DC was a constant. That beautiful brown face with the backward question mark blaze always made me happy. When I would ride him, especially at the canter—his most buoyant and animated gait, I sometimes would get the giggles because he was so exuberant and it was so much fun and I felt like a kid without a care in the world. Being on his back or in the aisle brushing him or standing around holding his lead rope as he grazed was priceless therapy. It's hard to feel lonely, bored, depressed, or sad when you are in the presence of such a powerful, lovely creature that is part wild and yet listens to you and can return affection.

He just had a full exam this July the week before

my wedding to see if the vet thought a 23-year old horse should be trailered from IL back to CA. She said, "He's in great health and he doesn't know he's 23. Keep working him. I think he'll be fine."

I had been trying to find a stable near my new house that would have provided him with an awesome environment for his golden years. Unfortunately my part of California is so heavily populated, there are virtually no barns with pasture turn out—or at least none I have found at this point.

So I'm happy to know DC's last days were spent grazing in a field with his horse friends in the Midwest. He was Kentucky-born and he belonged in a grassy pasture.

When I spoke to the hospital vet I thanked her and she said I should be happy I gave DC such a good home. "He was a Thoroughbred, right? Lots of those horses don't end up with a happy story with the same owner for so many years."

Maybe sometime down the road I'll be able to provide another happy ending for another noble Thoroughbred.

I'm grateful to have so many beautiful memories of my beloved horse. I even got a new nose thanks to him! :)

Attached is a picture taken at a horse show at

Lamplight from the summer of 2005. He really was photogenic and every bit as handsome as his show name "Adonis" suggests.

Thank you for reading this horse obituary. Thank you for being a special part of my past and present.

Love,
Susan

My friend Suzanne who had been there from the beginning of my time with DC responded almost immediately.

Susan,

Thank you for sharing your news about DC. I've got tears in my eyes; this could be my story with my horse. You expressed so many of the same feelings that I have about him. He too, has been a constant friend in my life. You could add up all of the costs and expenses of keeping them over the years, but their friendship is PRICELESS.

Although, there are a growing number of gray hairs on his forehead, he's in great shape and people are amazed when I tell his age. I believe regular riding, lots of big pasture turn out, and lots of TLC keeps him young.

Again, thank you for sharing... you'll see him in heaven one day. I honestly believe God's timing in amazing... you're now happily married and it was time for your dear friend DC to go. I guess I like to think of it that way.

Blessings and love.

My mom assured me DC's equipment was safe in their garage and next time I was home I could go through it—to donate what I didn't need anymore and hang on to the rest for my next horse.

"We can ship your saddle out to you, honey."

And so my brand new saddle—DC's saddle—took up residency in my garage hanging on the wall, just to the right of an old three-drawer file cabinet.

Every day I passed by the chocolate-colored saddle on my way to my car.

I shared quiet moments with the saddle every time I threw a load of laundry in the washer a few feet away.

This new forward-seat saddle had a cover on it so the dust wasn't apparent, but it broke my heart a little each time I caught a glimpse of it. DC's barely-used saddle served no purpose, and that was unbearable.

On a horse, a saddle is a portal to adventure, excitement, discipline, and friendship. A saddle without a horse is just a bunch of purposeless leather, an expensive ornament.

My saddle should have been in a beautiful tack room with other saddles and a long row of well-oiled bridles and gleaming bits, not displayed high above half-used paint cans and extension cords.

Even though it pained me to see my beloved and now deceased horse's saddle every day, it gave me comfort I was still a horse girl. I could be a horse lover—a full-fledged equestrian—even without a horse of my very own. That new saddle, now horseless, was my vision board in 3-D.

I still owned a saddle and one day I would have to make sure it served its purpose again. Sure it might take some time, but I was already very good at waiting. All those years of bad dates had taught me that at least.

I just hoped finding my next equine love would be faster and smoother than finding a husband. If I had to wait over three decades to start riding again, I didn't think I would survive.

Although, Her Majesty, the Queen of England, mounted on a Fell pony wearing a folded scarf on her head, made a compelling case for enjoying horses no matter your age.

CHAPTER 37

Finding My Handsome Knight

FROM THE MOMENT I swung my right leg over his back and settled into the seller's saddle, a certain little flutter descended on my heart. I thought this gelding seemed special and maybe, just maybe, he might be the one.

Having been on too many bad dates to count and more recently weird horse shopping expeditions, I didn't want to get my hopes up. Again.

After work and dinner with Mark I retreated to the office and scrolled through Dreamhorse.com. A few years earlier I'd scrolled through eHarmony; now that was just a memory. Everything had changed in my life, yet this quest for a perfect partner—equine version—made me feel like nothing had changed. Instead of going out on a string of disappointing dates where the guy talked too much about himself, bad-mouthed women from previous relationships, or was hard to talk to period, I entered a world of overhype.

During my first horse shopping trip, I met a cute, dark-chestnut gelding, but there was no chemistry. I liked him, but I didn't *like* him. Next, I met a gorgeous bay hunter who had a little too much vigor to be a pleasurable ride, pinning his ears over every fence as I watched my trainer test ride him. The seller admitted he was due for hock and coffin joint injections.

After that, there was the classy looking gray who ignored all my aids. He dictated exactly the rate of speed he felt he should be going at the walk, trot and canter—a total control freak. And then there was a very fun Paint. He had no splashes of white—just a solid bay—and he was really a cool horse, but he was shorter than the advertiser said. When I rode him, my legs dangled down his side. Of course the seller said, "He takes up your leg really well!"

I was discouraged I would never find the right horse. If I had a hefty bank account, the process of finding a new horse would have been so much easier. But in the price range I could afford, the horses were not completely sound, quite old, or too green. I poured out my heart via email to a barn friend whom I had met through DC about how difficult it was trying to find the right horse.

I'm still horse shopping. I wonder if you have any new thoughts on where to go/with whom to connect . . . I'm kind of stuck. Help!

She had read an article about a ranch for retired Thoroughbred racehorses that trained and transitioned them into riding horses. She told me I should give them a call.

I found the number online and called. A woman answered, and I poured out my heart again. "I am horse shopping and my last horse I owned 16 years until he died. I am a tall, rusty amateur who wants a horse that could do a little dressage, a little jumping—nothing big— maybe like 2'6", and some trail rides. I just want a fun horse I can dote on. I'm working with a trainer. And I'm partial to a bay with a blaze."

"I think I might have a horse you'd like. I'll send over an email." When the email showed up in my inbox, I leaned toward the laptop screen, read the message while waiting for the picture download to fill in.

This is a 7 yr old, 16.3h gelding. He is still green to jumping, but shows a lot of scope. He's doing 2'6" small courses right now, but no show experience yet. Very lovely mover, likes to hack with others, we haven't tried him by himself as of yet.

My eyes welled up with tears and I started to sniffle as the image of a horse that could have been DC's stunt double posed in a conformation shot with ears perked forward on my screen.

Dueling viewpoints fired salvos in my brain: First, *You can't go see that horse! You'll never find another DC and it won't be fair to this horse to expect him to be DC.*

The contrary thought shot back: *It's not fair to this horse to not go see him just because he looks like DC. You've got to give him a chance. It's just one more blind date.*

The second argument won and I asked my trainer to arrange a meeting to try one more horse.

THE SHORT TRIP from the mounting block into the arena felt familiar, and although I had just met this off-track Thoroughbred with the thick forelock and big eyes, when he cantered I was sold.

As an amateur rider who had not ridden regularly of late and had only started taking lessons recently after finding a young hunter/jumper trainer who taught nearby, my riding was pretty pathetic. My brain knew exactly what the various limbs of my body should be doing while in the saddle, but my dormant riding muscles could not execute.

Our canter transition was not smooth and there might have been some flailing on my part, but once this sweet bay boy settled into his stride, I smiled uncontrollably. Part of the smile stemmed from knowing I must have looked like a total dork, but the dominant part was I was having so much fun cantering around.

"Do you want to jump him?" asked my trainer, who had ridden him before me and after the seller.

"I'm worried I'll ruin him," I shouted to my trainer and the seller who perched atop chairs on the wooden platform next to the arena.

"Just ride him like he's your own," the seller encouraged.

"Okay, I'll do an X." I took an extra deep breath, stood up in the saddle for a second to try to force my heels down just a little further and shortened my reins.

Why did my mouth feel cottony?

I picked up a trot and aimed for the low point of the cross-rail. As this horse sprang over the small fence, my legs slid back and I forgot to give with my hands to release the reins so the bit wouldn't bump him in the mouth. The horse slowed down after he landed.

"That's good," I said, and joked about needing more lessons. I returned to trotting around the ring and with each step, the intensity grew. I knew I had to have this pretty, DC-look-alike horse.

MY NEW HORSE Knight contentedly munched his alfalfa. I brushed him with a green and fuschia Beastie brush and a soft brush. They had been DC's brushes. I didn't own a hoof pick or even a lead rope when we brought him home. My horse possessions totaled three girths and two Mattes pads, but zero hoof picks. And one lonely, almost-new saddle.

It was dark and not many people were at the barn. I didn't want to ride alone since we were still new to each other. I hand-walked my horse 15 minutes and he was better behaved than my dogs. Knight clip clopped alongside me and pricked his ears forward from time to time. A baby bunny shot out from the shadows and he didn't even acknowledge it.

I met a man hand walking a small chestnut horse. He proudly introduced me to his faithful companion of 30 years. "I bought him when he was 4. He's now 34. I walk him once or twice a day every day. I make sure he's getting enough water. He's got a good appetite, I just want to make sure he's drinking enough. I always look to see if there's a small splash underneath his waterer."

Next I met a woman in her 60s who introduced me to her black pony. "I always wanted a pony as a girl and I never had one until three years ago when I bought her."

I realized yet another thing I had missed about having a horse. Gentle, unhurried people who come to tuck their horses in at night. And the conversations springing forth during the tucking in hour.

The next night I rode Knight for the first time at home. It was dusk. My trainer made a special trip to the barn to help me ensure all my tack was fitting properly and lent a little moral support since were a new "couple." She had ridden him the day before and said he was great. Quiet, willing, no spooks.

I climbed the mounting block, hopped on, and settled in. We walked to the arena and a woman was in there with her turned out horse. She grabbed her halter and the horse shot across the arena, savoring his freedom.

And Knight just stood.

The little bunny returned and sat about 20 feet away, twitching its ear back and forth. Either Knight was aware and unconcerned or he was clueless there was a terrifying rabbit yards away.

I walked him into the ring and circled around; he strode forward on a loose-ish rein like this was his arena he had been ridden in his whole life. He seemed comfortable with himself. That was one of the qualities I really admired about Mark. After several laps I was convinced this was not a fluke—my new horse was a steady citizen, even in the dark, alone in a ring with small rabbits frolicking in the shadows.

I barely touched the sides of my calves to his barrel, and my new horse sprang into a trot. At first Knight was very forward, but as I posted intentionally slower, hesitating a bit longer in the saddle, he adjusted his stride to meet my desired rhythm. We shaped a few large circles into the arena sand and then changed directions. Knight seemed to be eagerly listening to my aids. I squeezed my fingers on the reins and stopped rising with the beat, and Knight transitioned to a walk.

I needed a breather since I had only been riding during weekly lessons. I both did and did not want to canter next. My mind flashed back to Daytona and how he'd buck when I cued to canter. I then remembered how DC would chose an end of the arena to spook at. Surely in this arena illuminated by only a few giant lights on towering poles, with very few other boarders around it was silly for me, an out-of-practice equestrian to think about asking a new horse—an ex-racehorse—to pick up a faster gait.

I bargained with myself I would canter and I only had to ride it out a few strides then we could descend to the trot. Gathering my reins again, I cued Knight to trot, sat a couple of beats, took a deep breath and squeezed the inside rein while pressing with my outside leg.

Knight sprang into a canter, bold and buoyant, rocking and rhythmical. No one was there to capture my grin, but it didn't matter. I knew in that November moment, in the stillness of a Southern California evening, with an audience of horses in their pipe corrals chewing bedtime hay, rabbits skittering at the arena's edge, here in this saddle with Knight I was home. And my prayers had been answered again.

Loose Ends

So if you're wondering what ever happened to Kevin from Chapter 1, the orange leather jacket guy: About five years after our miserable date, I noticed Kevin out of the corner of my eye at a church function. He didn't attend my church, so it was quite a surprise when he walked right up to me and said, "You know I just paid off that date we went on! It was $4,000 with attorney's fees and everything."

I didn't know what to say. It was such an abrupt greeting. My stunned silence was mistaken for a brush off because Kevin mumbled an apology and turned to walk away.

"Yeah, I remember. So how've you been? How are things going for you?"

"I just got married!" He held up his left hand flashing his ring.

"That's great. How'd you meet her?" I grinned, knowing I would not have to shy away from him for fear of him asking me on another hideous date. I was off the hook. Forever!

He beamed as he spoke of his new bride whom he'd known for years; apparently their friendship had taken a romantic turn.

Although *our* story did not have a happy ending, his story did.

I wonder if he still has the jacket.

Book Club Questions

1. How did Susan's early horse adventures with her best friend Gail compare to your horsey background?
2. What could have made Susan's relationship with her first horse Daytona more successful?
3. Which dating story did you find most outrageous or entertaining and why?
4. In your opinion, how is horse shopping like dating?
5. At what point in the Shane relationship would you have exited? What factors do you believe kept Susan entangled in this odd friendship?
6. What was the role of Susan's faith throughout the course of the story?
7. From falling off due to a too-heavy sled being attached to her waist to years later face planting and breaking her nose when her horse tripped, Susan had her share of riding accidents. What riding accidents have you experienced that were comical or not comical at all because you required medical care?
8. DC was Susan's heart horse. How would you define a heart horse and have you had a heart horse?
9. Do you view horses as God's apology for men? Why or why not?
10. Susan mentions in Chapter 35 "Too Soon for Goodbye" that life as a new wife and stepmom was difficult to navigate. In what way have you found life

or family challenges to be less challenging when you're with horses?

11. Knight, Susan's new horse, was a green off-track Thoroughbred. Have you ever purchased or worked with a green horse or an off-track Thoroughbred? Share what you've learned from your experience.

12. If you were to write your own horsey memoir what would you title it and why?

Author's Note & Contact Info

Thank you for reading! In case you were wondering, this book shares stories from my horse life and romantic life as I remember them. I have changed names to protect the privacy of some of the people involved. I used dialog at times to communicate the essence of a conversation, even if I couldn't recall exact wording.

One other thing—I would love to connect with you! Here's where you can follow along and find me:

- Email susan@saddleseekshorse.com
- Receive my email newsletter to stay in the loop saddleseekshorse.com/sign-up
- Read my blog Saddle Seeks Horse saddleseekshorse.com
- Like the Saddle Seeks Horse Facebook Page facebook.com/SaddleSeeksHorse
- If Instagram is your jam instagram.com/saddleseekshorse

If you enjoyed *Horses Adored*, it would mean so much to me if you would leave a review on Amazon or Goodreads. Reviews are gold for authors! They allow more exposure to new readers. And word-of-mouth recommendations are wonderful too. Thanks for being so kind!

I hope you enjoyed my stories and are right now creating some of your own with a very special horse.

Tally ho!

Acknowledgements

First, thank you Mom for all your prayers and encouragement. I know you always wanted a pony, but hopefully you've gained as much joy from Daytona, Chassy, DC and Knight to have made up for "riding" the wooden fence around the cow pasture. I couldn't have done any of this without you. For all the hours at the barn, horse shows and those cold winter nights when you went to feed the horses in the dark . . . you deserve a halo! I can tell from every print out of each new blog post you place in a manila folder that you are my biggest fan. And I am your biggest fan too.

Dad, I'm so sorry for all the times my barn clothes made you sneeze! I am grateful for your support of my horse craziness from taking me to Arlington Park as a kid, to dropping me off at Cindy's farm to cutting out every horse-related newspaper article you find. Fourteen hundred kisses are headed your way.

To my beautiful sisters Linda and Renee and the bros-in-laws and world's best nieces and nephews, hugs and kisses. I'll try not to smear lipstick on you.

Joanne, you are a gem and the most honest, fun, expressive horse trainer I will ever meet. Your hospitality, warmth, and excellent communication are legendary and without you, much of this story wouldn't exist! Thank you for helping me find my heart horse DC. I adore you!

Gail, Heidi, Beth, Carolyn, Dana, Patrick, Ramona, Suzanne, Amy, Vanessa, Holly and Holly, Carly, Raquel,

Carey, Heather, Isabelle and Kasia. You are exceptional people and I'm honored to call you my friends.

And to my Gal Pals, I'm so glad we have formed a horsey community together.

Beta readers, you know who you are! Thank you for taking the time to read through all these stories. Without you there might not be a completed project. Kudos and blessings to you all.

And to all the friends and friends of friends who ever let me ride your horses, I cannot thank you enough. Much love.

Since this book was released in 2018, the man of my dreams decided I wasn't his dream anymore, leaving our marriage in order to (his words) "follow my bliss." That heartbreak story is for another time. If being an equestrian has taught me anything, we horse girls are resilient and after a fall, we *always* get back up. By keeping this love story alive in book form, available to readers, I'm metaphorically back in the saddle, my home, riding with eyes up and an open heart.

Let's Stay Connected!

You're invited to stay in the horsey loop with me.

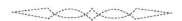

Trot along on the blog where I
share equestrian information and
inspiration for horse lovers like us.
Visit the link below to subscribe.

saddleseekshorse.com/sign-up

Tally-ho – Susan

Strands of Hope

How to grieve the loss of a horse

Through personal stories, interviews and practical tips,
find strands of hope for the bereaved equestrian.

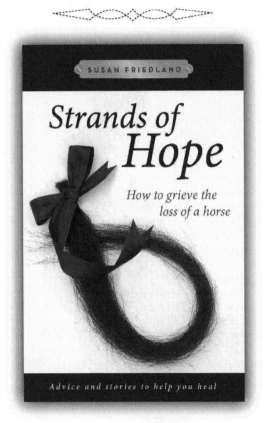

68778969R00182